BONANZA PUBLISHING

Thelma

Wild Horse Rider

Rick Steber

D1041842

BONANZA PUBLISHING
Box 204
Prineville, Oregon 97754

Printed by
Maverick Publications

To Kristi.

"Ah, she's a great old life, she is. To show you ... I was born here'n Wallowa Valley, in a log cabin. When I was a boy, wasn't no railroad, wasn't no cars.... I've lived a different kind of life. I was lucky, I broke horses, rode rodeos and street carnivals.... Everything's changed to where it just don't seem possible.... When I'm dead and gone, I'll be dead and gone. Just like I was never here at all."

Lew Minor
1912 World Saddle Bronc Champion
Pendleton, Oregon

PART ONE

CHAPTER 1

L ight pushed dark.
The Seven Devils gradually accepted the glow of
the moon and at Hells Canyon the moving line of light
jumped from one rim to the other without ever touching
the Snake River a mile below. A few wispy clouds,
shredded by the granite peaks of the high Wallowas,
began to blush a delicate salmon pink that lingered for
a moment and changed with the emergence of the moon
to a chilly ice-blue. Ice-blue reflected off the mountain
snowfields, downward to the moraine lake and beyond
to the skinny valley running north-south.

A horned owl perching in a towering pine shifted its
weight. The first few wing beats were audible, then
silence; field mice scampered to hide from the passing
shadow. There was another rustle of wind, the
impression of feathers stroking the air, as the owl
landed in a fir tree outlined by the rising moon. The owl
spoke four distinct notes, the first two in rapid succes-
sion and the others drawn. Its voice filled air ripe with
blooming camas and wildflowers, drifted across the
meadow and through the fingers of timber to touch the
log cabin.

Jennie Minor closed her eyes and listened to the owl
talk. It helped to distract her until the contractions
began once more and then beads of sweat appeared on
the delicate blonde hairs of her upper lip. The rhythmic
tick of a mantle clock counted time. She squirmed, cried
out in pain from between clenched teeth and her

husband William rose and came to stand beside her. The soft creaking of his rocking chair slowed and then ceased and Jennie's breathing returned to normal.

At the apex of the moon's broad arc, light began pouring through the distorting pane of the west-facing window illuminating the stark white of the sweatsoaked sheet. It reflected off the dresser's oval mirror and bounced around the room to four chairs pulled tight to a table, a dull-black cookstove and a row of pots and pans hanging from nails driven in the header log.

Clouds passing over the moon cast intermittent shadows on the cabin and the bald-faced hill tucked behind. A scant wind shimmered tall grass on the hillside and a band of unnoticed horses grazed over the crown and down the cabin side.

Birds began to chirp and sing as the eastern sky colored and William interrupted his monotonous rocking and returned to Jennie's side. He spoke in a soothing tone, "You'll be all right," and then more formally, "Better do chores. I'll open the window. If you need me I'll hear."

He raised the latch and pushed open the window, noticing the mountains as he did. "The mountains look especially beautiful, so bright and fresh." He hesitated. "Jennie, the baby will come when it wants. Best save your strength for then."

William closed the door solidly behind him and drew a deep breath that filled his lungs with the fragrance of morning. He exhaled and built-up tensions flowed through his neck and cascaded off his shoulders. This was a good day to be alive. He started in the direction of the barn knocking dew from the grass with his boots. Milk pails swung at the ends of his arms.

On the hill the wild horses came alert. The stallion, a big strawberry roan, positioned himself between his mares and the only sign of civilization for miles, the log cabin and barn. His eyes followed William across the barn lot until he disappeared inside and then the horses returned to grazing.

William finished chores and emerged from the barn. He noticed the startling quiet as if the world were drawing a long breath. The barn door slammed shut. A meadowlark sitting on a corral post twirled a simple melody. Blackbirds called raucously back and forth in the willows. And then a new-born cry split the air. William dropped the milk pails, sprinted toward the cabin and milk drained and was absorbed by the soil.

The stallion snorted angrily from flared nostrils, threw his head and chased his little band of mares over the hill biting the rumps of the slowest. A line of dust hung suspended to mark where they had been as the golden sun peaked over the horizon.

On this date, Friday the 13th, July 1884, in Wallowa Valley, Oregon, Lewis Minor was born. The wild mustang was no longer without master.

CHAPTER 2

At one time the Wallowa Valley sat at the bottom of a great inland sea but a gigantic upheaval thrust mountains through the earth's crust and the water receded. Trees sprouted. Salmon spawned in the free-flowing rivers. And a race of red-skinned people, the Nez Perce, came to inhabit the land.

William and Jennie Minor were among the first white settlers. They claimed homestead land in a broad meadow near a spring and built a log cabin facing the Wallowa Mountains which rose in an awesome sheer ascent beginning, it seemed, at their very doorstep.

It was a February day in Lew's seventh month when Jennie left him alone, asleep on a blanket on the floor, to hurry to the spring for a bucket of water. The spring gushed into a crystal pool and even in winter watercress grew there. Jennie dipped a bucket and bent again to break loose a few green clumps of watercress. As she shook moisture from the leaves she thought about the salad she would fix.

Following the trail through the snow to the door the mountains called attention to themselves, their white bluntness against the steel blue of the sky. An icicle that had lived all winter on the eaves of the cabin lost its grip and crashed to the ground, shattering. Jennie pushed open the door and froze, motionless, horror-struck. Lew, on hands and knees, was teetering on the fireplace hearth.

"Stop, Lew!" she commanded but at the sound of

her voice he turned, lost his balance and pitched headlong into the orange flames. Jennie saved him, scooping him from the fire, and brushed away a live coal which had imbedded itself in the delicate skin of his forehead. Her baby whimpered but did not cry.

CHAPTER 3

William, in long underwear, lit the oil lamp. He dressed and crossed the room to where Lew, now four years old, lay asleep on a cot. He noticed for the first time his son's hands, the fingers long and thick like his own. He almost hated to awaken the boy, his facial expressions lost in sleep, but gently and yet firmly he took Lew by the shoulders and shook. Lew struggled to open his eyes and his tongue licked over dry lips.

"Time to get a move on. Can't sleep the day away — not if you're goin' hunting with me."

For the past several months William had been promising to take Lew hunting "one of these days." That day was here and Lew slipped out of bed and started pulling on clothes, stuffing a flannel shirt inside trousers without bothering to unbuckle the belt.

William reached high to remove the Winchester rifle from its spot on the antlers above the door. Outside on the trail to the barn William instructed Lew, "Remember, stay quiet and close, but not too close. I won't want you steppin' on my heels."

The large man and the small boy passed the barn and cut diagonally across the meadow toward a prominent finger of timber. Lew exaggerated his stride trying to place his feet exactly in his father's footsteps and having to stretch to do it. They were almost to the dark canopy of the forest; William imagined a deer struggling to its feet from a bed beneath a fir tree when his fantasy was interrupted by Lew's stumbling and stubbing his toe on a rock.

William turned, spoke in an earnest whisper. "Watch it. Be quiet now."

They entered the trees. William paused and Lew took the opportunity to backhand his runny nose with the sleeve of his coat. William moved again and Lew followed blindly behind. He concentrated on watching where he placed each foot and would not have seen a deer if it were standing beside the trail.

William lumbered along like a bear, choosing where he stepped but not conscious of it. He was a big man of uncommon strength. A drooping eyelid gave his face an air of uncompromising determination.

The floor of the forest smelled heavy and damp with toadstools, mushrooms and pine needle duff. And then it happened. Lew took his eyes off the trail for only an instant and in that instant he stepped on a dry twig and it cracked like a shot.

From somewhere ahead came the distinctive thump-thump-thump of a deer going out. William dropped to one knee. A doe stopped and looked over her shoulder, curious and unafraid. William's rifle recoiled and barked instantaneously and a bullet splattered on a rock outcropping just in front of the doe. Before another shot was fired Lew flung himself on his father pleading, "No, Papa, no! Please don't shoot the little colt."

The deer disappeared and William moved to discipline his son but seeing his distress he relented. Effortlessly he raised Lew to eye level. Patiently he explained. "Son, I know you have a fondness for horses but every animal you see is not a colt. That was a deer. We needed the meat."

CHAPTER 4

L ew sat at the table anxiously watching his mother press five small tallow-dipped candles into a chocolate cake still warm from the oven. She lit the wicks and turned to the table, the flickering flames played across her face. As she set the cake in front of Lew, William reached under his chair, slid out a package and placed it on the table. Lew's eyes widened. He wanted a pair of cowboy boots so badly he could taste it. The box seemed about the right size and for the moment chocolate cake was forgotten. He reached for the box.

"Just a minute, Lewis," reprimanded Jennie. "First you have to make a wish and blow out your candles."

Lew took a quick gulp of air, unleashed a miniature windstorm. Then he tore open the box and stared at his first pair of cowboy boots, copper-toed with a red star inset on the uppers.

The next morning Lew awoke early. He was excited not only because he would be able to wear his boots the entire day but also because he and his father were going to be branding. It would be Lew's job to keep the branding fire hot.

Lew stood in the center of the corral, wood smoke curling around him. He had a sudden impulse to see what it would be like if he used tobacco and drew a breath of smoke only to choke on it; coughing, eyes watering, he decided it would not be good.

"Get it hot," called William. Lew tossed a pitch knot

on the coals and when it caught fire he laid the branding iron across it. William waded into the herd of milling cattle swinging a lariat. The loop snaked out and settled over the head of a calf. William stood his ground and reeled in the calf like a big catfish on a hand-held line and when the little bull was standing spraddle-legged in front of him he reached around it and flipped it upside down. With his own weight he pinned the fighting calf to the ground.

"The iron," he commanded. Lew brought him the branding iron and stood by to watch as red hot metal touched hide and a flash of fire singed hair. Lew's nose curled involuntarily at the stench but he watched, absorbed and yet coolly removed. William reached in his pocket for his jackknife, opened it, slit the scrotum in a quick half-moon slice and dropped the warm, alive testicles into a Mason jar. Afterward, they would cook the Rocky Mountain oysters in a fry pan over the branding fire coals.

Instead of turning this newly-made steer loose William allowed the animal to gain his feet and then held him while he told Lew, "Hop on. Give a ride."

Lew straddled the calf, his father let go and as soon as he did the calf commenced bucking. Natural instinct told Lew to dig his red star boot heels into the calf's ribs and for a few exhilarating seconds he was riding but then the calf bucked him off. It took a moment for senses to catch up and when they did Lew felt pain in his elbow. He spit out a mouthful of dirt.

Lew was between the mother cow and her calf and the cow dropped white-tipped horns and started a swift charge that was stopped by William stepping forward and giving her a whack across the bridge of the nose with the stiff lariat. She whirled, stood a short distance away pawing at the ground and bellowing until her calf found her.

"You okay?" asked William, coming to give Lew a hand.

Lew's elbow was bleeding from a small cut. He still had not regained his breath but he rasped, "Catch him for me, will ya, Pa?"

That night, long after he should have fallen asleep, Lew was still awake reliving the sensations of riding the calves; the loose skin shifting under his grip, the contractions and explosions of the animals' muscles, the sense of weightlessness and above all else the thrill and exhilaration.

CHAPTER 5

Joseph, chief of the Wallowa band of the Nez
Perce, led a small party of braves mounted on
dark-bodied appaloosa ponies. Lew, up in the hayloft,
spotted them first and called to his father who interrupted the evening milking and stepped outside. The
Indians rode directly toward him.

William was inwardly surprised to see them. Since
the war the Indians had been confined to a reservation
in Oklahoma but lately there had been talk that the
tribe had been transferred to the Colville reservation in
eastern Washington state. William had never been a
participant in the war, did not fear the Indians now.

"You friend," said Joseph, carefully measuring each
word. As he spoke to William he was aware of the boy
at the window above. "Me, you, have no trouble. I old.
Want place here valley, die. You sell me land? You
help?"

"If I were the only farmer it might be different,"
began William, "but I'm not. There are others to consider. Since the war no one wants you as a neighbor.
There are hard feelings. I am only one man. What can I
do?"

Joseph fully comprehended the rejection, spun his
horse and he and the others galloped away across the
meadow and into the timber. Lew watched intently,
asking himself why they could not be neighbors and
why the Nez Perce were excluded from the valley. They
had lived here in the old days but he had seen Indians

13

only five or six times in his entire life and then they were Umatilla or Cayuse who came over the mountains to hunt and not members of the proud Nez Perce. Lew jumped from the loft onto a pile of loose hay, slid onto the ground and went to where his father had resumed milking. He said to his father, "Why won't anybody sell them land? Didn't they used to own it all?"

William stood, shoved his hat back on his forehead and looked long and hard at his son. He raised his drooping eyebrow, stroked his mustache and said, "Boy, I think it's time you got some book learnin'. When school takes up I want you to go."

The school was two miles over the hill and up a tree-less draw. It stood by itself and occasionally a cow would wander by the log structure, stretch a long neck and stare in a window. When this happened giggles would ripple across the room until Miss Coffin, the teacher, would rap her ruler on her desk top.

One afternoon at recess the children were playing Annie-Annie-Over. The ball cleared the ridgepole and came bouncing off the tamarack shakes. Lew was standing directly in the path of the ball and he caught it and started running. At the front porch he went to plant his foot, expecting to cut sharply around the corner, but his feet went out from under him and he slid, from boot to belt, through a fresh cow pie. The laughter of his classmates erupted around him and Lew jumped up and made a dash for the barn.

Miss Coffin rang the bell to signal the end of recess. Lew heard it but continued to scrape dung from his trousers with handfuls of hay. Eventually he returned to class and slipped into his chair. Miss Coffin tried to ignore the disturbance, the snickers and scraping of desks and chairs being slid across the floor away from Lew, leaving him an island.

Miss Coffin walked to Lew; his heart was thumping

14

but he did not look up at her. She realized he was a strong-willed individual and given to outbursts of temper. She had broken up fist fights between Lew and older boys several times in the past. Lew was big for his age and that only compounded the problem. She placed a hand on his shoulder and said, "Sorry, Lew, but accidents will happen."

As the center of attention Lew blushed and the vein on his forehead stood out. For a moment he endured and then he leaped from his chair and ran from the room.

Jennie was in the cabin kneading bread dough and reflecting on the day she and William had come into the valley when her daydreams were interrupted by the sound of a horse coming hard off the hill. She glanced at the mantle clock. It was much too early for Lew to be coming home. She stepped to the porch. It was Lew, riding her gentle saddle horse at breakneck speed down the steep incline. To see him riding so fast — one stumble, a badger hole — frightened her and she cupped hands and shouted, "Lew, slow down," and when he was closer, "What's wrong?"

Lew and the horse barrelled past her standing on the porch, flour on her apron, fear still etched in her frown. He tossed over his shoulder in passing, "I ain't goin' back!"

He stayed in the barn a long time, rubbing foam from the mare with a gunny sack. When his mother called him to dinner he went reluctantly, sat at the table but piddled with his meat and potatoes, eating very little and remaining quiet.

In the morning, about the time Lew normally would be saddling his mother's horse, he was in the barn pitching hay to the stock. William was feeding the hogs. Nothing was said until Lew restlessly blurted, "I'm not going."

William ignored his son but when he finished feeding he turned his attention to Lew. In a matter-of-fact voice he said, "I been watchin' you here as of late. You can do anything you want when it comes to a horse. That's a God-given talent." He paused and then resumed his well-rehearsed speech. "I got a proposition for you. You pick out a colt and he's yours."

"For my very own?" Lew queried cautiously.

"Yep, but now the other half of the proposition is, I want you back in school." William took hold of Lew's shoulders. "Do we have a deal?"

Lew excitedly shook his head yes and then tore away running toward the pasture. He already knew which horse it would be. Charley, a white gelding.

CHAPTER 6

Lew turned fifteen and in the month since school let out he had grown a full half inch taller and his muscles were becoming more defined. He was fast changing from a boy to a young man and from sunrise to sunset he spent his time in the corral pitting his new-found strength against the wild temperament of the untrained colts. Sometimes Jennie, dish rag in hand, stood on the porch watching and the raw wildness of the action in the corral alarmed her. She wanted to march over and put a stop to it but did not dare.

Lew learned how to ride bucking horses by being thrown, often times unceremoniously, and each evening he came in with a new assortment of black and blue marks, scrapes or cuts to show for his effort. One night Jennie told her husband, "Lew is the most determined person I ever heard of."

"Naw," replied William, "just hard-headed."

By the following summer there was no boy left in Lew. He had become a man; his voice was lower and at William's suggestion he was shaving.

In a wild horse band leadership is exerted by the most dominant animal. But dominance is measured by more than strength, aggressiveness and fighting skill; a leader also has an undefinable element of character and like the mustang leader Lew was developing that brand of character.

As he gained maturity he identified closely with the instincts of the horses he was training. He perceived that the horse's most basic instinct is to run away from danger and he used this knowledge to his best advantage. His training technique started with haltering a colt. A colt who fought the halter would be snubbed to a post with its front legs hobbled. This blocked any chance to flee. Some animals went berserk at the restraint but soon learned there was no advantage in trying to match Lew's strong will. He gained their respect through fear and intimidation; once gained the teaching process would begin.

One day a neighbor sat on the top rail of the corral watching Lew work a particularly rank colt. When Lew took a break the neighbor said to him, "When you get done playing around with these colts you might be interested in trying your hand on a real horse. I got a stud at my place that could give you an education."

"Bring 'im on," said Lew, quick to accept the challenge.

With a knowing grin the neighbor departed and returned leading a high-spirited coal-black horse. Lew threw open the gate and the stud ran around the confines of the corral, making tight circles and alternately pawing and kicking at the air.

The day was hot and Lew had rolled up his shirt sleeves exposing sinewy forearms to the sun. As he watched the horse he removed his Stetson, a birthday gift that he had shaped buckaroo-style, and ran his fingers through his hair. He wiped his forehead and crushed the hat back on. He took a rope down off a post.

The corral was Lew's domain. He stood in one spot allowing only his eyes to follow the horse's movements. He did not trust the high-spirited horse but even when it came past him, hindquarters swiveling and kicking, Lew did not flinch.

In the heat the black horse began to sweat and white flecks spotted his deep chest. On the next pass Lew tossed a loop that settled squarely over the proud black head. He moved fast to take a dally around an anchor post. The stud fought the rope, jerking back and rearing. At one point while the stud's front feet were pawing the air Lew yanked on the rope, the horse lost his balance and crashed to the ground and in the same instant Lew had crossed the distance between them and was in command, sitting on the horse's head. The animal thrashed about wildly and when he quieted for a moment Lew tied his feet together with a lariat loop. With the horse so restrained, Lew began his attack, whipping off his shirt and using it to slap and rub the head and the horse was trying to fight, squealing and snorting. When it was over and the horse would fight no more, Lew stopped, freed the restraints. It was a few minutes before the horse could struggle to its feet and stand, tremors racking its body and a mix of sweaty foam and dirt marring the blackness.

Lew had not allowed the neighbor to watch the training. Several days later when the stud's owner returned he found Lew in the barn. "See he ain't kilt you, yet. What's the matter, lose your nerve?" There was sarcasm in his tone.

"You know better. I said I'd take care of him and I did. Want to see what he can do?" asked Lew coolly.

Lew saddled and when he mounted, the big stallion did not even roll his eyes. With only the slightest amount of pressure on the reins Lew took the horse through an intricate series of figure eights, brisk cuts and abrupt stops. He finished with a flurry and dismounted.

The neighbor stared, mouth agape. All he could find to say was, "I can't believe it. I just can't believe it. Nobody's ever rode Diablo."

Diablo helped boost Lew's reputation as a horseman and others began bringing horses by for him to train.

Some were spoiled, some jugheaded and a few were plain outlaws. Lew devised teaching methods to suit each type of horse; kickers might be discouraged with a club, strikers with a well-placed boot toe; but always the punishment fit the crime and the offender immediately associated anti-social behavior with pain. Lew operated on the principle of punishment and reward. Oftentimes the reward was simply to stop the punishment.

CHAPTER 7

Wayne Wade, a man from the lower valley, rode into the Minor homestead and Jennie stepped to the porch to greet him. "Good day, Mr. Wade. I'm about to set dinner on the table. Care to join us?"

"Thank you," Wade tipped the brim of his hat in her direction, "but I'm in kind of a hurry. I would like to speak to your son, if that's all right."

"Of course. If you change your mind it won't be any trouble to set another plate. You'll probably find Lew around the barn."

Lew stepped from the tack room and extended his hand to Mr. Wade. Wade shook hands with him and was impressed with the confident grip of the young man. Lew was eighteen, six foot three and a solid two hundred pounds. His high cheekbones and prominent nose appeared chiseled of stone but the cowboy hat pushed way back on his head gave him a youthful appearance.

The two talked about meaningless things, the weather, hunting, fishing, until Lew finally interjected, "You didn't ride all the way out here to make small talk. What's on your mind, Mr. Wade?"

Wade chuckled at Lew's directness and replied, "You're absolutely right. Some of the boys are planning a county fair and asked if I would talk to you. They've got a rodeo set, fifteen dollars prize money for the best ride, and thought you might be interested. You have to furnish your own saddle and bucking horse."

"Where would I get a horse? Everything in this end of the valley is broke plum gentle," Lew said cocksure.

"I've seen that white horse you call Charley. He may not be young as some but take it from me, lock him in the barn for a week and pour the grain to him and I guarantee he'll come out bucking. You can win on that horse."

The day of the rodeo Lew rode another horse and trailed Charley to Enterprise. He arrived early and sat off by himself in the shade of a cottonwood tree, surveying the scene and sizing up the other riders as they arrived. It was apparent he would be one of the youngest contestants but his confidence was unshaken. He knew what he could do. If there was any doubt it was that Charley would refuse to buck but Lew had stopped on the way, picking a burr for insurance.

As the afternoon wore on, sun and dust boiled like syrup over a hot fire and the list of riders was reduced to only a few. Then it was Lew's turn. As he saddled Charley the sun slid behind a cloud and lost most of its punch. Two fellows off to the side passed a bottle of moonshine between them. A fat lady pulled a shawl over newly discovered sunburned arms. Lew tugged the cinch tight and tucked his insurance policy, the burr, under the saddle blanket. Outwardly the only nervousness Lew displayed was a slight tightening of his lips. He squinted as the sun ducked between clouds and led Charley to the center of the arena. Charley was skittish, sidestepping and prancing, and Lew did not know if it was merely the crowd or something more. He spoke to Charley, petting him, soothing, reassuring. He checked the cinch one last time, it was tight.

"We're ready when you are," called one of the judges.

Lew snugged his hat down, drew a deep breath, gathered the reins and swung into the saddle. He grabbed a deep seat and his spurs dug into shoulders with a shock that triggered Charley's explosion. The horse erupted in a four-footed leap so high off the ground the crowd drew a collective breath. A kid selling peanuts stopped to watch and the plunge began. Hooves hit the ground like pile drivers and gave Lew the sensation of having his head driven down through his shoulders. Spurs gouged and raked. Charley put distance in his next effort, twisting and turning.

Lew was in no position to observe the small boys who quit shooting marbles and crowded in close to the mesh wire to watch. He did not hear the cheering crowd, was aware only of himself and Charley. The ride was so wild and exhilarating that he threw his head back and whooped at the top of his lungs.

One instant he would be weightless and the next crushed into saddle leather, spun this way and back around the other, but ultimately Charley faltered and stumbled, After that his heart was no longer in it but Lew stayed with the spurs intent on draining every last ounce of energy Charley possessed.

When it was over Charley stood in the center of the arena, drenched in frothy sweat, trembling, and Lew became cognizant of the standing ovation of the crowd, the stomping feet on the bleachers and he gave them a showy wave and dropped to the ground. His chaps slapped against shins as he strolled toward the gate and Charley tagged along behind like a puppy following at heel.

Other contestants came to shake Lew's hand and offer congratulations. There was no doubt that he had won and as soon as the program was complete Lew was awarded the $15 prize money. On the way home that day one man told his son, "A lot of men go a lifetime without witnessing the exhibition you saw today. That ride was something you'll remember the rest of your life.''

Several days after the rodeo Wayne Wade made another visit to the Minor homestead, this time to talk business with Lew. He asked if Lew would be interested in going to work for him running a herd of cattle on Devils Washboard. The Washboard was hilly country, rough as one would imagine the devil's own washboard to be, and so remote and rugged no rancher had attempted to run cattle there. Lew took it as a compliment that he should be asked, that he should be first.

''I don't know where you'll find water and you'll probably have trouble with bear and cougar but I'm in a real tight bind. With this hot weather all the grass down here is already gone, burned up. What do you say, can you help me?''

Lew talked the proposition over with his parents before notifying Wade that he would accept the challenge. A day later, riding Charley and leading a pack horse, Lew started the Wade cattle toward Devils Washboard country. He drifted them slowly scouting around for the best grass and adequate water.

Each day that summer Lew cared for the cattle but there was not much actual physical work involved so he took it upon himself to build a one-room cabin. Using an ax he felled trees, stripped the bark and cut the notches. Singlehandedly he lifted the logs into place. The cabin was situated in a gulch near a spring and provided a relatively luxurious camp until September when the grass in the surrounding area was eaten down.

Lew decided to move the cattle to the upper end of the Washboard but first he had to establish a steady source of water. He spent several days searching and all he could locate was a moisture seep along a rock wall. He tied a rope around a tree above the cliff, lowered himself over the edge and used a pick to bring enough water to the surface to form a pool at the base of the rock. When cottonwood leaves turned bright yellow and danced in a wind that threatened snow Lew started the herd back over the Washboard toward Wallowa Valley. Occasionally a deer mixed in for a mile or two before stepping aside.

Wade met Lew and he and a couple of his hired hands took over and drove the cattle the last few miles to his ranch. Lew returned home. The following day Wade made a special point to ride over to the Minors' homestead and tell William and Jennie they had every right to be proud of their son.

"The calves are big and healthy and the cows fat as cows get. I don't know any man who could have done the job Lew did," he told them.

For several days Lew helped his father catch up on projects that required two men, built a new hay derrick, loaded grain and took it the five miles into Wallowa.

One evening in the middle of chores William called to Lew, "I hear someone comin'."

"Okay," answered Lew but he kept busy doctoring a colt in one of the barn stalls.

Two men appeared on the opposite side of the stanchion where William was milking. He recognized them and called a greeting. "Well now, Johnny and Hec McDonald. What you boys up to?"

The McDonald brothers were successful Wallowa businessmen. Their current venture was to gather wild mustangs in the hills and sell them to a U.S. cavalry buyer. Johnny, who was not much older than Lew, was the wheeler-dealer and Hec more the orderly professional. It was Johnny who spoke first. "I was down to Enterprise, seen Lew make that ride and without a doubt I would have to say he's the best bronc rider in these parts."

Lew, listening to the conversation on the other side of the wall, smiled as he rubbed ointment on a gash on the colt's leg.

"We could use his talent breaking remounts but thought we better check with you first to make sure it would be all right to talk...."

"We have a signed contract to deliver cavalry remounts," injected Hec. "We spent the last four months gathering 'em and now we need a bronc rider to trim down the rough edges, else the Army'll reject 'em. We'll pay top dollar...."

William held up his hand as a signal for Hec to stop and said, "Save your breath. You don't have to convince me. Lew's the one to make arrangements with. You'll find him in the horse stall, other side of the alleyway."

It was Johnny who explained what was needed to Lew and Hec who outlined the financial details. Lew answered, "I'll have to check with Pa. He might need me around here. We got to get the wood in and button things up for winter, you know."

William's voice boomed, "It's your decision."

"In that case," said Lew, turning his attention to the McDonald brothers, "when do I start?"

"First thing in the morning," Hec told him. "Come to the red barn on this end of town. I'll have someone there to wrangle for you."

After the deal was sealed with a handshake Johnny and Hec brusquely left, afraid Lew or his father would change their minds. Lew was not about to. He danced joyfully in the stall.

"That colt actin' up?" called William.

Lew stopped, called back, "Just a little." He was grinning and unable to hide it.

Early the following morning Lew sprang from bed and lit the lamp. Before his mother and father were even awake he had fed the stock, saddled Charley and was headed to town. He rounded the hill and started to ford the river when two squawking mallard ducks rose from a back eddy. Charley's ears perked and he followed them with his eyes as they made a lazy circle and came over in a low pass. Lew pretended to shoot at them and at an easy gallop urged Charley toward town.

George McNeese, one of McDonalds' hired men, was waiting in the big red barn for Lew. He was curled up in the hay catching a little extra sleep and grumbled when he had to extricate himself from his comfortable, warm spot. Lew pulled the saddle off Charley.

"Where do I start?" asked Lew and George told him as he pointed to a corral of horses, "Makes no difference, you got to ride 'em all and a lot more to boot. Pick one and I'll put your saddle on 'im."

"In that case, " said Lew, motioning to a small bay mare, "I might as well start with something easy and work my way up. She looks about the tamest of the bunch."

The mare was saddled and bridled and George brought her to the bucking area, a freshly plowed triangular piece bordered by the barn, the Wallowa River and a millrace. As George watched Lew check the cinch and prepare for the ride he suppressed a knowing grin because this particular little mare was a stick of dynamite and the fuse was burning.

The mare's response to weight on her back was to drop her head and swap ends but despite this bit of fancy footwork Lew remained firmly in the saddle. The little bay went temporarily insane, bucked over against the millrace, found the narrow footbridge, went over it and continued bucking recklessly down Main Street.

At the George Holme residence Mrs. Holme was seated in a comfortable chair in a bay window enclave reading a book. She had not the slightest inkling that the mare, in one tremendous buck, had cleared the boardwalk and fence and was coming around the side of the house tearing down a clothesline loaded with her undergarments. As she flipped a page peripheral vision caught movement and she glanced up, shrieked and tossed the book. It looked for the world as though a horse and rider were coming through her window.

The horse changed directions in mid-air and, dragging the line with Mrs. Holme's personal things, continued on to knock over a row of two-year-old fruit trees along the side of the house. Once gain the mare cleared fence, boardwalk and all, and landed back in the street. Lew was having a good time of it, whooping and hollering, and shoppers and store owners came to the doorways to watch.

A half-hour later Lew returned, the horse at an easy canter, completely under control. George jumped up from his spot in the hay and with a know-it-all grin said, "Sure glad you picked something easy to start with."

The last horse that day was a gangly sorrel that bucked into the Wallowa River where it reared and went over backwards. Lew kicked himself free, grabbed the horse's head and shoved it underwater. By brute strength alone he held it there while four feet pawed the air to a frenzy. George was watching and feared that Lew was going to drown the horse but at the last moment Lew pulled the head above water. The horse, with fight still remaining, lashed out with his teeth trying to bite. Under he went. This time when Lew let him up the fight was gone.

Lew rode six days a week, one horse after another and he never seemed to get enough. But one morning, with a steady downpour of cool rain, he decided to knock off and let the storm pass. He climbed into the haymow and slept. When the rain stopped beating on the tin roof he climbed down and instructed George to saddle him a horse.

Uptown at the barber shop the barber was sitting in his own chair facing the window and the street, waiting for a customer. He watched women in long skirts step around mud puddles and teams of horses pulling wagons plod on through when he saw something that forced him to cry out, "Jesus Christ!" There was Lew Minor on a bucking horse and the horse had slipped in a mud puddle and was falling. Lew landed on his shoulder and somersaulted.

As soon as Lew hit the ground he knew the shoulder was broken; he heard a bone snap. The horse got up and ran off. The barber and several others who had witnessed the accident rushed into the street and tried to help, but Lew growled at them, "Leave me alone, I'm all right." He walked to the doctor's office, had the arm placed in a sling to immobilize the shoulder.

Lew was out of commission for three months while the shoulder healed. During that time he was short-tempered, gruff and moody. Finally, impatient at waiting for the doctor's go-ahead, Lew went out, found a horse with a mean streak and it was like he started to live all over again.

It was a wonderful spring morning and Lew was riding into Wallowa from the home place when he was overtaken by a man. Lew saw him coming and pulled up.

"My name's Wren," the stranger informed Lew.

"You're from up in the Butte country. I've heard the name."

"That's right," replied Wren. "Stopped by your folks, they said you was headed for town. I want to talk; got seven hundred head of horses and I need a fellow like yourself to green break 'em. I got to the middle of July and then they go out. Pay'd be twenty bucks a month and I'll take care of room and board, put you up at the Mitchell Hotel in Joseph.''

"I'm interested, itchin' for a little excitement."

"I could use a couple bronc busters if you know someone else that can ride."

"Might. Friend of mine, Orv Hearing, just lives up the river, rides a pretty fair lick. I could see if he's interested."

"Fair enough."

Orv was two years older than Lew, of average height and weight and regarded as a good horseman, although his star never shown as brightly as Lew's. He jumped at the chance to ride for money.

During the weeks spent in Joseph breaking Wren's horses Lew and Orv were inseparable and became very best friends. Their personalities complemented each other; where Lew would shout and holler on the very best rides wearing his emotions clearly on his shirt sleeve, Orv was always under control and reserved. Sometimes Lew would fly off the handle but Orv never lost his temper. Lew was carefree, raw, green; but Orv, with those extra couple years, was mature and seasoned.

Lew always rose first in the morning. He would run fingers straight back through his hair, pull on his hat and be ready for a bronc for breakfast. Orv dragged himself out of bed and never went anywhere before first shaving the stubble from his face and waxing his handlebar mustache. Then he would have a big breakfast. He took whatever time it happened to take that particular morning, never rushing it.

By mid-July Wren's horses were green broke and ready for shipment. Lew and Orv helped drive them the fifty miles over the mountains to the railhead at Elgin.

After it was over and the horses safely corraled, Lew shucked his shirt to beat the dust out of it and the muscles across his back rippled with open aggression. He wore an orange bandana around his neck for a little color and he removed it to wipe his face. When he finished he was grinning. "Wasn't it great! God, I had fun! We had some goddamn rides, didn't we? Probably never get that many good horses together again, least not around these parts."

"Yep." Orv looked a little forlorn. "Wish there was some way me and you could stick together but I don't suppose there is."

"We make a hell of a team, don't we?" Lew maintained his grin for another few seconds and then it hit him that the two of them would most likely be separating. He grew thoughtful. "You know, Nevada has a million head of mustangs. That's what I've heard. Imagine." He began to warm to an idea. "A million mustangs running free and wild. We could go there. Me and you. We could catch on busting broncs until we pulled a grubstake together and then chase mustangs. There's money in mustangs."

Orv's dark eyes widened as he contemplated the possibility. He spoke with well-measured words. "That's an idea. Ain't no hooks holding us here. Suppose a fellow ought to get out and see the world while he's young enough to enjoy it."

"Damn right," affirmed Lew and becoming more intense all the time, "Can you imagine the bucking horses! Out of a million head there has to be some mean sons-of-bitches mixed in. I'd give anything to have a go at 'em."

Lew and Orv, without reaching a solid decision, started back for the Wallowa Valley. They had crossed the mountains and were in the canyon, riding side by side, when Lew off-handedly demanded to know,

"Well, Orv, we going to do it or not?"

"What's that?"

"Come on." Lew's aggravation was like a flag run up a pole. "Are we going to Nevada or not?"

"Are you positive we could find a job once we got down there?"

"For Christ's sake yes. There's always a market for bronc busters. Nevada's the place for us — Nevada — where men are men and the horses are wild. All I know is I'm goin'."

"Well then, I'm going, too," shot back Orv. "We're a team, remember?"

Lew was grinning. Orv was not.

CHAPTER 8

L ew invested $40 to have George Lawrence build a sturdy swell-forked saddle to take to Nevada with him. The evening before he and Orv were to depart he sat on the porch of his parents' cabin polishing the leather and trying to imagine wide open sagebrush flats. He was sure Nevada held his future.

In the morning Lew kissed his mother goodbye, shook hands with his father. Jennie cried and William told him to take care of himself and then Lew was gone. He planned to leave Charley in town and William would bring him back to the homestead later for safekeeping in case Lew ever came home.

Lew and Orv already had their tickets; they would take the stage from Wallowa to Elgin and travel by rail from there. The train was late arriving in Elgin and Lew was impatient. He kept looking down at his new saddle lying at his feet wishing it were on a mustang's back somewhere in Nevada while Orv felt the first twinge of homesickness.

In LaGrande they transferred from the branch line to the main line and a day later arrived in Salt Lake City where they had a layover before catching the westbound train.

It seemed to Lew that he had been riding in the confining, rattling, smoky railroad car forever and he complained to Orv, "God, I'm sick of this. What say we get off at the next stop, I think that'll be Winnemucca, and check things out. We can always catch another train.''

Orv was tired of the travel, too. ''Suits me.''

Winnemucca was located in an enormous valley along the Humboldt River. The only trees, willows and a few cottonwoods, grew along the meandering river; grass grew on low spots and stunted sage on the drier ground. Orv spotted Canadian honkers on a sandbar in the river and called attention to them but Lew looked beyond and exclaimed, ''Horses! See 'em?'' For a while a band of running horses, kicking up a cloud of dust, stayed parallel to the tracks but eventually the train outran them and they turned up a draw.

Winnemucca consisted of a depot near the river and streets running up a gradual hill. As Lew stepped from the train he inhaled the fresh air and stretched sore muscles. A man approached selling cherries but Lew shook his head no while Orv bought a cup and gave them to a small girl he had visited with on the train.

At the hotel the clerk behind the counter, who saw cowboys every hour of the day, took no real notice of Lew and Orv until they started up the stairs to their room. Then he glanced a second time because rarely were cowboys Lew's size.

In the room Lew pulled on spurs, buttoned the conchos and gave the sharply pointed rowels a preliminary spin. The metal sang and Lew paced back and forth listening to the jingle-jangle. Orv stood in front of the mirror combing his hair. Lew glanced at him and announced, ''You as hungry as I am? Let's go get a bite to eat.''

On the way Lew stopped at the desk and asked the clerk, ''Say, if a couple of fellows was lookin' for a bronc bustin' job where would they go to find one?''

''Today is Saturday, the foremen of the big outfits come in on Saturday. Swing by Stockman's Bar. That's where you'll find them." The clerk added emphasis by snapping his red arm garter.

Lew and Orv ate first and then stopped at Stockman's. The bar was crowded with vaqueros and buckaroos in dusty hats, most still wearing chaps and spurs. There were also railroaders in striped overalls and a few Basque sheepherders off by themselves at a table.

"What can I get you?" asked the bartender, wiping the counter in front of them with a beer-soaked towel. Orv told him, "Shot of whiskey," but Lew said nothing. The bartender addressed him, "How about you?"

"Nothing."

"Nothing?" As the bartender moved away he mumbled to himself, "Hell, he's big enough to eat hay and drink out of the ocean and he don't ...?"

"Doesn't it ever bother you to be in a bar and be the only one not drinking?" asked Orv.

"I tried it once but I didn't care for the taste. A man shouldn't have to drink somethin' if he don't like the taste."

A short squatty fellow sat at a table by himself sizing up Lew and Orv. After Orv's drink came he wandered over and introduced himself. He said he ran a cattle ranch and was looking for a couple extra hands, asked if they would be interested in going to work for him.

Lew looked down on the top of the man's balding head and disgustedly told him, "We're bronc busters. We're not interested in punchin' cows."

After the man returned to his table Orv was mildly upset that Lew had thrown away their chance of employment. He took a sip of whiskey before saying, "Don't I have a say?"

Lew regarded him skeptically. "What ya mean?"

"He was offering us a job. You and I should have at least discussed it."

35

"Naw. Hell, we're bronc busters. I ain't comin' all this way to play nursemaid to a bunch of shitters." Lew gazed around the crowded room and caught the attention of one of the working girls. She began making her way toward him. Before she got there a man stepped up and introduced himself as Sibble Reed. He alternately puffed a fat cigar and talked.

"Ain't seen you boys around here before."

"We're from up in Oregon." Lew wished the man would step aside. He had lost track of the girl.

Reed took another puff and continued, "I'm foreman of Double Square, biggest horse outfit in the country. Run ten thousand head. You boys bronc riders?"

"What ya think?" Lew was a bit put off by the question.

"I think you may be, but then again you might not. Hard to tell unless, of course, I see you on a horse and then I'll know in a hurry. Wouldn't you say?"

"You damn right you would," Lew bristled.

"I don't need another ordinary bronc buster, they're a dime a dozen. I want a man, or a couple of men, that can crawl on any bronc I got and ride him. And I need someone who can get along with my buckaroos. That's why I never hire someone I don't know will fit in. No drifter comes in a full-fledged bronc rider for Double Square. I start new men at thirty-five bucks a month at the bottom, as wranglers for the cook."

"Not me," hissed Lew. "I don't have to wait to be a bronc buster, I already am." And remembering Orv, "And so is my partner."

"Didn't mean to insult you, just that I got to make sure a man fits 'fore I make him a buckaroo. That's the way it is. Work for me and you start at the first rung on the ladder."

"Bullshit," scowled Lew and turned his back to Reed.

"If you change your mind look me up. I might be able to use a man with a little backbone," said Reed and walked away.

Orv wanted to say something, to tell Lew he was acting a fool but thought better of it and remained silent. It was a part of Orv's character that when he was angry he would allow himself to cool down before saying anything.

Presently a gentleman wearing an unblemished tan derby stepped forward and commented, "I'm sorry but I couldn't help overhearing your conversation and quite frankly I am in need of bona fide horse trainers. Am I to understand you are qualifed along that line?"

Lew sneered, "Does a bear in an orchard shit peach pits? Ain't no horse I can't stick with."

The man introduced himself as George Webb, a businessman from Lovelock, sixty miles down the line. His proposal was $10 apiece to have mustangs turned into saddle horses.

Lew knew a good deal when he heard one, could not suppress an arrogant grin as he extended his hand. "Mr. Webb, you got yourself a deal."

Lovelock, a cluster of railroad tie houses and false-fronted stores, made a small dot on the vastness of the high desert. The Humboldt River flowed through town, went a few more miles before disappearing into a sandy sinkhole. Coming in on the train Lew yearned for the horses he would have the opportunity to ride, itched for the chance while Orv, comparing the flat horizon to home, longed for the intense blue of the Wallowa Mountains. Here the colors were muted, softened by grays and tans and subtle shades of yellow and brown. And the vastness of the flat terrain momentarily depressed him. Why, a man could ride hard as he could and at the end of the day still look back and see where he had begun.

Once they debarked the first order of business was to check into a room at the hotel. Orv was unpacking, putting clothes away in the dresser when Lew, who had been stretching on one of the beds, suggested they take a stroll down to Webb's corrals to have a look at the stock. With an airy attitude he mentioned, "Think I'll take my saddle, never know when you might find somethin' you want to ride. Besides, I haven't had a chance to break it in, wanna see if it works."

Lew carried his George Lawrence saddle slung over his shoulder to the corral where he lifted and set it on the top rail. George Webb came up while he and Orv stood eyeballing the spirited horses that swirled the dust as they raced back and forth across the corral.

"Are you going to ride?" he asked Lew.

Lew said nothing. His concentration was focused on a leggy chestnut stallion with a white mark on his forehead. He stepped between rails, took a lariat off his saddle and began shaking it out.

In short order it was apparent he was after the chestnut and Webb remarked to Orv, "That's an ornery horse, name of Spotlight. No one has ever ridden him."

Spotlight was well-muscled with a powerful gait and as he swept past Lew roped him and at once Spotlight reared and Lew nimbly took a wrap around the snubbing post. Orv pulled the saddle off the rail and started into the arena while Lew walked down the taut rope hand over hand, caught hold of Spotlight and roughly eared the big horse down. The saddle went on and the cinch was tightened around a heaving belly. They were ready. Lew let go of the ears and bounded into the saddle.

A glint of late afternoon sun broke on silver spurs, diffused into a whirl of motion as rowels gouged horsehide and set off a detonation. The first few jumps were heaven high, straight up and back down, all in the same spot. Spotlight must have comprehended such antics would never unseat this rider because then he plowed ahead foolhardily throwing himself into full-scale war. To Lew the sensation was disjointed and there was always the driving jolt as hooves pounded ground.

"My God!" wailed Webb, covering his mouth with his hand. The action was so fierce that he almost hated to watch, but watch he did, peering through the rails. Across the street on the boardwalk a woman turned away abhorred at the spectacle.

Spotlight, gone berserk, gathered himself and tried to clear the fence. He did not make it, landed on the top rail and it cracked, splintered and gave way; so did the second railing. Spotlight was balanced, as much out of the arena as in and Lew, God damn his ornery hide, was still spurring.

In the days ahead Lew and Orv worked George Webb's horses and for extra money, sometimes only for the fun of it, Lew rode exhibition on Lovelock's main street. Local ranchers brought in the worst-tempered horses they could find and Lew took fiendish delight in riding and entertaining; flailing the horse with his cowboy hat, silver angora chaps rising and falling to the staccato beat of the particular devil horse whose spirit he was breaking.

They had been in Lovelock exactly one week when in the middle of the night came an urgent knock on the door. Orv, not wanting to be disturbed, pulled a pillow over his head. Lew groaned, rolled to his side and groaned again as he sat. Another sharp rap and he was awake. Grousing, "Hang on to your hat. Jesus Christ, just a minute," he pulled on his trousers and walked barefooted and shirtless to the door, opened it to see the smallish silhouette of George Webb outlined there.

"What time is it?"

"Four o'clock." Even at this early hour George was

dressed impeccably, his derby had been freshly brushed but standing there in the dim hallway his brow was wrinkled into a frown. He looked worried. Lew invited him in, struck a match and lit a lamp.

George began at once, not waiting for the soft light to find all the corners of the room. "The audacity of that animal. He steals my horses. What insolence."

"Hold it now. What are you talking about?" Lew's irritation showed through like a beacon in the night.

George, a little more settled, explained. "A half hour ago a wild stallion came in, knocked down a section of fence and ran off every horse I own." He lamented, "They were already sold." Wringing his hands emotionally, he insisted, "You have to go after them and bring them back. You must. Everything I own is tied up in those horses. They have to ship out this week."

Lew, foot propped leisurely on a chair, arm resting on thigh, remained stoic. It seemed to George that Lew was enjoying some sort of contemptible pleasure in seeing him squirm but he pleaded, "Please."

His personal decision made, Lew snapped to attention and announced, "I'll take off as soon as it's light." George, much relieved, departed hastily.

Lew finished dressing, threw together a bedroll and left Orv sleeping with his head still beneath the pillow. Downstairs Lew ate a big breakfast of scrambled eggs, bacon and thick sausage gravy over hot biscuits. He also asked the cook to make him a half dozen sandwiches to take along.

Along the slow-moving Humboldt River a cool mist gathered like wool on the bottom strand of barb wire and as day began to break the polyphony of frog and cricket voices began to diminish their serenade. By the time the sun pushed gold-rimmed clouds off the horizon Lew, mounted on Webb's personal saddle horse, had waded the river and was headed north across the flat that stretched without fence 150 miles to the Oregon border and beyond. Ahead of him jackrabbits dashed from one clump of sage to another. He kept the horse to an easy canter following the tracks left by forty shod horses driven by one that was not. Over his shoulder the rising sun warmed him but as it continued its arc the heat made him sweat. Several times he removed his hat and wiped his brow on the go, never permitting his mount to stop but sometimes allowing it to walk.

Early in the afternoon a smally puffy cloud germinated into an ominous thunderhead that engulfed the sky. Compassionately the storm blocked the fierce sun whose intensity had been doubled by reflecting off the white sand. In places little eddies of wind obliterated the tracks and on those occasions Lew kept headed in the general direction, swinging left and right until relocating the sign.

In time rain began to fall, a brief, cool torrent that opened tiny holes in the sand. Then, as quickly as it had struck, the rain moved on leaving the desert alive with the tingly, fresh perfume of rabbit brush and sage; rocks steamed and gave off an identifiable fragrance all their own.

The storm moved east and the setting sun discovered a slot of open sky and dropped in it. Feathered fringes of cloud effervesced a barrage of color from yellow to red and the entire spectrum of orange. The light began to fall as Lew climbed a narrow trail tight to the side of a steep butte. On top he eased over a rimrock lip and could see the horses milling around out in the open. He guessed the trail he had just followed was the only way off the flat-topped knob and set up his camp in a commanding position.

Nearby was a small spring amid a grouping of house-sized boulders. A fence of woven sagebrush had been fashioned between boulders and it was evident that sometime in the past buckaroos had used it to capture wild horses. Lew formed a plan as he allowed his mount to drink thirstily from the cold water.

Without the energy of the sun the basalt rocks began to surrender their heat and blue-bellied lizards moved to fissures where they would stay warm through the night. Lew started a small sagebrush fire, the flames popping, snapping and casting a cheery glow on his tired face. He half wished he knew how to play a mouth harp. There was too much silence.

To the east a rich slice of moon melted away the clouds and stars appeared shining brilliantly, a coyote tested the air with a string of yips. Lew was in place, pressed into a crevasse between boulders within easy reach of a gate that would seal the fence around the spring. He knew the horses would be in for water sooner or later and he waited.

A palomino stud with a free-flowing mane and tail appeared almost white under the moonlight. He kept the other horses back as he tested the air. A trace of wind was blowing toward the spring and the stud could not catch scent of Lew and kept coming. Finally the horses belonging to George Webb sensed the water and their thirst could be restrained no longer; they rushed headlong for the spring and began slurping. The stallion was confused, whinnied but he, too, finally came in. Lew waited until he was drinking before sliding the pole across to close the gate. The stallion whirled, reared and was met by a lasso loop that dropped cleanly over his head. Lew tied him off short to a stout juniper then, rather than excite the other horses anymore tonight, he shook out his bedroll and slept the few hours until daylight.

Morning on the desert is normally reserved as a time of silence and solitude but that morning was interrupted by the distinctive popping of saddle leather as Lew urged the palomino stallion to buck. They went at it for a good fifteen minutes and it never entered Lew's mind that he could be thrown or the horse could lose its footing and he would be left injured, miles from anywhere. Within an hour the palomino, which had once in the distant past been a saddle horse before running away and becoming an outlaw, was under Lew's control. He rode the horse herding Webb's band back toward Lovelock, seventy miles away.

Lew delivered the horses that evening and they were loaded directly into boxcars. As Lew pulled his saddle off the palomino, a big stout horse that seemed to fit him perfectly, the train whistled and steamed off into the darkness. Later Webb come to the hotel to tell Lew and Orv, "You are the finest men I ever employed. I hate to give you leave and hope you do not mind but I took the liberty of wiring Mr. Reed. He wired me back that his offer remains open."

Lew snarled, "I ain't no wrangler."

Nothing more was said about the standing offer until later when Orv was able to pragmatically maneuver the conversation back to the subject of the Double Square. He said it was his opinion they should seriously consider it and he carefully listed the benefits, concluding, "Ten thousand head, Lew. Think of the broncs." Lew wrestled with his pride against the realization that the only time he felt absolutely alive was when he was on a bronc and he and the horse were giving it their all.

"Suppose we could mosey back toward Winnemucca. If we happen to run into Reed we can talk. But I'll tell you one thing, I ain't kissing his rear just to work for him."

Lew and Orv rode horseback along the road that roughly paralleled the rails. Every few hours a train, going east — going west, chugged and rattled past. Overhead a row of clouds along the horizon broke off singly or in groups of twos and threes and migrated across the broad expense of deep blue sky.

At one point, rather than having to follow the road out and around a hill they followed a trail that went up and over the brow and dropped down on the other side. As they broke down on the flat valley floor once again they found a homesteader's sod house; three ragged little kids and a pet antelope came out to gawk.

Lew and Orv rode in hoping for a drink of water. The homesteader, a scruffy type in his thirties but looking fifty, invited them for dinner, explaining, "We ain't havin' much but we got plenty of it. You're welcome."

Lew had to duck his head as he went through the low doorway and it took time for his eyes to adjust to the dimness. It was refreshingly cool inside. Lew began to make out the almost ghostly apparition of a woman at the cookstove and remembering manners he removed his hat. He could see her well enough now to notice she wore a plain skirt and a white blouse and when she turned to say hello her voice was light and soft and her face was pretty. She turned back to the stove and busied herself stirring a pot of beans. Lew pulled an apple box against the wall, sat down and leaned back. He scrutinized the woman and asked himself what kind of life this would be. She was still a nice-looking woman but in a few years she would be old and used up. Married and settled down would never be his kind of life. He wanted to go where he wanted, when he wanted and stay as long as he wanted. Feeling momentarily sorry for her, he commented, "What you got cookin' smells mighty good." She flashed a warm, fresh smile on him, opened the oven door to expose several loaves of delicately browned bread that she removed and set on top of the stove to cool. Speaking to the men she announced, "You might as well be seated, the kids can eat later."

After dinner, as the men were going out to sit on the porch and enjoy a bit of a cool breeze that had begun to blow, Lew again complimented the woman, saying the beans and warm bread had been, "Right tasty, ma'am." The kids stampeded for the door and the chance to eat but Orv headed them off, gave each an Indian head penny and they acted as if it were the only personal money any of them had ever possessed.

Lew and Orv climbed back in their saddles and continued on, spotting the twinkling lights of Winnemucca well after dark. They raced the last few miles and Lew's palomino was far and away the faster. They tended to the horses, putting them up at the livery before finding a room and getting a bite to eat at a family-styled supper house. Afterward, when Orv said he was in the mood for a drink, Lew said he would go back to the room and stretch out.

Orv walked straight to Stockman's, found an open spot at the bar and ordered whiskey. He took a perfunctory sip before noticing he was standing beside Sibble Reed.

"So, back in town. Heard you might be. Your partner still with you?"

Orv nodded, took another taste of whiskey and rested his elbows on the bar. Reed seemed preoccupied, spoke in a prosaic tone. "I know just what makes your partner tick and maybe you, too. It's those wild broncs. They get in your blood...."

Reed paused to lick and then light a cigar. He puffed vigorously to make sure it was going before removing it and continuing his one-sided conversation. "I know all about it. I had the disease. But a man gets married, has kids and the fire sort of leaves you. And every year it takes a little longer to heal. Anyhow, that's the way it was with me. Used to live and die for those broncos. Not no more." Again he paused, this time reflecting, and then continued. "Well, how about it? Want to sign on?"

Orv rolled the last swig of whiskey around the bottom of his glass like a miner panning gold. He spoke to that rather than directly to Reed. "I'll have to talk it over with Lew." And by way of explanation, "We're partners."

Reed caught a reflection in the bar mirror and snapped toward the door. Lew stood there, feet slightly apart and firmly planted, hands on hips and looking like he owned all he surveyed. He wore a cowboy hat, an orange bandana around his neck, a yellow shirt and boots and silver spurs. Reed sighed, remembering the times he felt so brazenly on top of the world. There was something about being the best, looking to prove yourself, that made the attitude rise to the surface. Call it cockiness, conceit, swell-headed arrogance or plain old confidence. Lew had it all. One look and it was a challenge. "Go find the worst bucking horse you can find, bring him back and I'll ride him."

Lew spotted Orv and swaggered over. Reed stuck the cigar back in his mouth, smiled and said, "Just been tellin' Orv I'm in the market for a couple good bronc busters and underline good." He removed the cigar and used it as a pointer. "You two may be the ones I'm lookin' for. I don't know. So far all I've heard is a lot of windy talk from George Webb. He says you boys done him a good turn. I don't know, hell, it might be nothin' but a crock of shit. He ain't a horseman.

"Tell you what I'm willing to do. I'll start you at thirty-five a month plus room and board and if and when you demonstrate to my satisfaction you measure up I'll bump you to seventy-five.

Orv got the inevitable question out of the way.

"Would we still have to start at the bottom?"

"Damn right." Reed was indignant. "I say a man worth his salt don't mind wrangling to start out. You'll get your chance and if you measure up you move up.

"Tell you what, I see a fellow over there I got to talk to. Why don't you boys talk it over. I'll be back."

Lew turned and hunched over the bar, allowed time for Reed to walk away and slammed his palm on the polished wood surface. He steamed. "Me wrangle for some hard-assed cook. No way. Get this. Get that. Fetch me water. Not for me, no sir."

Orv tried to sooth. "Well now, I suppose we ought to at least think about it for a minute. Face it, he needs buckaroos a lot worse than he needs wranglers. This is our chance, seventy-five dollars. By spring we'll have our own outfit and be running mustangs."

"I don't like the idea one goddamned bit."

"But Lew, remember what he said, Double Square is the biggest outfit in the country — ten thousand head of horses."

"Yeh but ...." Lew was thinking, thinking about the worst of the ten thousand. Sure, probably all of them would buck but some small percentage were going to be demons and that thought ground at his soul.

"Let's give it a go. We can always walk away if it gets too bad," offered Orv, trying desperately to find the right inducement. He wanted, needed, a steady job; needed the reliance of a regular pay check and the security of knowing what he was going to be doing the following day. He could take the bad with the good, wrangling for a cook was not beneath him.

Lew grumbled to himself. "Horse shit on a shingle."

Reed returned and in a cheery disposition asked, "Well, you boys made up your minds yet? Want to come to work for me?"

"On one condition," drawled Lew, "that you don't

wait too long to give us a chance. We're bronc busters and not fond of the ground.''

Reed's manner abruptly changed and he belligerently thumped his chest with a thumb of the hand that held the cigar. ''As of right now you're working for me. We'll have a drink. Bartender, get us three down here.'' He turned to Lew, ''What'll you have?''

''Nothing. I don't drink.''

Reed jerked back in surprise, shook his head from side to side appraising Lew. ''You're the first. Never heard of a bronc buster didn't drink.'' He gulped his own drink and as he departed he emphasized, ''You got tonight and tomorrow off, but first thing Monday morning make sure you're at Double Square headquarters, up above Midas. And come ready to work.''

CHAPTER 9

Noon Sunday Lew and Orv departed Winnemucca riding north at a leisurely pace; they planned to camp over and go in to headquarters early in the morning. Paradise Valley stretched before them. In the distance were hills dotted with dark green scrub juniper. Scrawny jackrabbits and deadly rattlesnakes were the only creatures living on the valley floor. Every so often a frightened rabbit hopped erratically away but the snakes had hidden from the heat of the day wedged under rocks or in the shade cast by a friendly sagebrush.

They rode without talking across the length of the uninterrupted flat and began climbing into rolling foothills, each seeming higher than the last. At the convergence of two draws they found a trickle of water and decided to make camp. According to the directions they received in Winnemucca, the headquarters of Double Square would be just over the next ridge. It would take an hour in the morning to get there.

That evening, as the sun was sliding into the far off Pacific Ocean, the coyotes smelled food cooking and came in close, occupying high points and yipping and howling. Orv did not mind except he felt a prick of loneliness, he always did when he heard them. Tonight they bothered Lew, got under his skin enough that he finally pulled his rifle from the scabbard and fired several shots into the air.

At the first hint of dawn they broke camp, the

palomino leading the way up the long rocky slope. They topped out just as the sun peeked over the distant chain of mountains. To the north was the powdery blue of another range of mountains and stretched out between was the uninterrupted, subtle tones of the high desert. In contrast, directly below, was a hidden valley, green and grassy and standing water reflected like turquoise on a green velvet mat.

Lew pulled up, rested a forearm on the saddlehorn. "Ain't it a shame to ruin a pretty mornin' like this." Then with a touch of spurs the palomino broke over the top and started down the other side.

On the floor of Starr Valley the grass was tall enough to brush Lew's boots. He sat straight in the saddle, fingers of the right hand gently holding reins, determining direction by the slight pressure of his thigh. The big palomino moved easily and with grace as horses bearing the Double Square brand broke left and right. Lew rode with prideful arrogance. He was not a defeated man coming in to surrender and be a wrangler — he was still a bronc buster at heart.

The headquarters of Double Square included a stone main building and wood barn surrounded by fifteen or twenty tents, some big enough for only one man and some set up for two.

Lew and Orv rode directly to the main building, dismounted and tied their horses to a hitching rail. Lew took each stair, seven of them, one at a time and inside where it was dark and shielded from the rising sun, they came across an old man mopping the floor. He mopped back and forth over the same patch of floor like the repetitive motions of a machine. He wore an abused and dirty silverbelly Stetson that should have been thrown away years before. Lew stopped him by asking, "Where do we find Sibble Reed?"

The man leaned on his mop and drawled, "Well

now." He took the time to remove a bag of tobacco, separate a paper and roll himself a cigarette. He struck a wooden match with a fingernail and lit the cigarette, exhaled a cloud of smoke and finished his answer. "I can't tell you. I don't rightly know."

"We're the new men he hired, supposed to check in with him and get lined out," clarified Orv.

The old fellow showed a toothless grin. "You boys startin' to work here ya don't need to talk to Mr. Reed. Your business is with Soggy, he's the cook. You'll be wranglin' fer him." He chuckled. "You're in fer a treat.

"Ah hell, Soggy ain't a bad sort but let me give you a little advice. Don't cross him — cross him and you'll have a fight on your hands."

It seemed the old man never had a chance to talk and was making up for it now. "Soggy's just a nickname. Don't know as if I heard his God given name, probably couldn't remember if I had. He's a Chinaman, hell for stout in his day and a real vaquero. Worked for Pete French, don't know where all else. Can be a temperamental son-of-a-bitch when he wants but bet he couldn't weigh more 'n a hundred and twenty pounds even if he was standin' in the river."

There was a scuffling in the kitchen as someone came inside, and then a scratchy voice with a foreign clip asked, "You ramebrains suppose be my wrang'ers? If so better get here, fast."

Lew and Orv exchanged glances. If the old man had not laughed Lew might have stayed where he was or walked out the door. Instead he followed Orv to the kitchen.

Soggy, a jumpy little brown-skinned Oriental, his graying hair pulled back in a cue, started by detailing what he wanted done and what he expected of his new wranglers. "I put water on, bring outside to barn when hot.''

Lew cursed himself for signing on but dutifully carried the hot water outside and toward the barn. As he stepped through the doorway Soggy's unpleasant voice, like fingernails grating on a blackboard, demanded, ''Give me hand.'' Lew set down the pails and helped roll the chuckwagon to daylight. Lew took a step back to inspect the wagon; the canvas top was dusty and full of cobwebs. A chicken, interrupted on the nest, got up squawking and hopped to the ground where she complained and criticized. Lew would have liked to have wrung her neck.

Orv came out with two more steaming pails. Soggy used them to splash the interior and sent Lew and Orv back to put on more water. With a fresh bucket Soggy scrubbed the grub box and the shelving of the letdown, using a pocket knife to clean around the nail heads. He was thorough to a fault but after a dozen pails he said that was enough water.

''Hate see grown men nothing do.'' He pointed to Orv. ''You grease harness,'' and to Lew, ''You big man, you bring boxes.''

Lew packed cases of canned goods, sacks of beans, coffee and flour, smoked sowbellies and cooking utensils to the wagon and handed them to Soggy. Never did Soggy say thanks, if he said anything at all it was to criticize and Lew slowly burned. When all the things had been transported Lew expected they would break for dinner but they did not. When he finished one chore Soggy had another waiting: fill the woodbox, fill the lanterns with lamp oil, shovel chicken manure. Orv took his time at his single task of greasing harness, made the job last until finally Soggy declared, ''Fix meal. You go now. You come in rater and wash pot, pan. Then you eat.''

After dinner and after the dishes were washed, Lew

and Orv retired to a tent. Lew was annoyed and vented his anger swatting at the horse flies that buzzed around.

Along toward dark the buckaroos came drifting in from all corners of the range. Lew and Orv ate supper with them, a group of leathery-faced men who ate in silence, and afterward, while the men sat outside on the steps smoking and jawboning, Lew and Orv washed dishes, pots and pans. By the time they finished, the others had retired to their tents and Lew and Orv did the same. Lew fell asleep in short order but Orv lit one cigarette after another, smoked and thought about the coming clash between Lew and Soggy. That it was coming was a foregone conclusion, it was only a matter of time; might be tomorrow or the next day. If Reed would only keep his word and promptly give them a shot everything would be fine but if he did not....

There was very little to the night as Soggy flipped back the tent flap at 3 a.m. and began barking instructions. He wanted the fire started and he wanted a box of personal effects carried to the chuckwagon and the horses had to be harnessed and the list went on and on.

Lew and Orv were allowed to eat breakfast with the buckaroos. As the men got up to leave, Sibble Reed came in and poured himself a cup of coffee. Soggy addressed Lew and Orv and told them to snap to it, to collect and wash the dishes. Lew wanted to ask Reed to give a chance to prove himself but was embarrassed by the soap suds on his forearms.

Reed told Lew and Orv, "Might as well leave your horses here. You can ride in the wagon with Soggy. But bring your saddles — a fellow never knows when he's going to get his chance."

The men rode out followed by the chuckwagon. The aged man stood on the porch and watched. When they were gone he returned to the dining room and, talking nonsense to himself, mopped the floor again.

Lew reclined in the back of the wagon, stretched out across the tops of oat, bean and flour sacks. He hated the rocking, jolting motion of the wagon and the confining canvas cover. He would almost rather walk. Orv sat on the seat with Soggy and went out of his way to make conversation.

"How'd they get to callin' you Soggy?"

"First time cook biscuit, no good," Soggy told him.

"Tasted all right to me. In fact, I thought they were down-right good."

"Thank you for the compriment."

Lew resented Orv talking to the man, said to himself that Orv should have more loyalty. He noticed the way his friend tugged at the ends of his mustache and it irritated him each time Orv did it. Finally Lew pulled his hat low over his eyes and made a solid attempt to block everything from his mind.

Soggy was in a talkative mood. "I rode Pete French, long time. We were buckaroos. You boys never know how that be."

Lew did a slow burn of resentment, mumbling to himself. "Where does that bastard get off saying Lew Minor will never know what it's like to be a real buckaroo? Hell, I've been a bronc rider and I been a buckaroo all my life. I can ride any horse God put down on this ol' earth. Damned if I can't. Why won't Reed give me a chance." And a fine layer of dust settled over his unmoving frame.

There was beef steak and mashed potatoes and hot biscuits served for dinner and afterwards Lew and Orv packed water and washed dishes. Twice Soggy rejected plates Lew had washed and both times Lew's neck flushed deep crimson. Somehow he managed to keep the cap on his unstable temper.

After the chores were complete, Lew went to the fire

and dried the dishwater from his hands and arms. Orv rolled a cigarette and sat down to smoke it. Soggy was out of sight, puttering in the letdown. One of the buckaroos, a lanky fellow wearing a dusty black hat came over and sat on his haunches by the fire. He recalled how tough it was when he started with Double Square and was forced to endure Soggy and wrangling.

"Give Soggy a chance," he ventured. "Out here besides a cook he's the doctor, the barber, he'll mend your trousers and he'll pull a tooth if it gets to aching."

"He may be a lot of things," said Lew, purposely raising his voice, "but likeable ain't one of 'em. In fact, that damn Chinaman ain't nothin' but a first class asshole."

The second day's routine was the same as the first. This time they made camp on the bank of Mullican Creek and in every direction, as far as the eye could see, were small clouds of dust from mustangs on the move. Lew was carrying in an armload of sagebrush for the fire, wondering what chore Soggy would next find for him when Soggy asked Lew to break a horse out of the remuda and shoot a couple of rabbits to sweeten the stew. Lew was only too happy to climb on a horse and he went quite some distance from camp before even looking for a rabbit.

He returned with two rabbits gutted and skinned. Soggy smiled friendly-like and surprised Lew by saying, "Maybe I be too tough on you. Want no bad feering." And he presented Lew a freshly baked pie. It was still warm to the touch and Lew held it in his hand, staring at the thick flakey brown crust, cocking his eyebrow the way his father used to when he suspected something. Without a word of thanks he took the pie over to where his bedroll was spread on the ground. He sat and made sure Soggy was not looking before using his knife to peel back a section of crust. An unappealing stench burned his nose and he pulled away. Soggy, in pure meanness, had made a pie filling of onion skins, potato peels and horse apples.

Lew left the pie on his bedroll and strolled over to the fire where he sat on his haunches and waited until the buckaroos drifted in and gathered around for supper. Soggy was busy making biscuits, popping them out of the dough with an empty tin can. Lew slipped over to his bedroll and got the pie, carried it behind his back until he was almost to Soggy and when the cook turned around he shoved it in his face, ground it in and walked away.

"Stop right there! Put it down!" commanded Reed and Soggy stopped dead in his tracks. Lew continued on and calmly took a seat on the ground by the fire opposite the direction the wind was blowing the smoke.

Soggy slowly lowered the butcher knife he held over his head with two hands. Only a moment before he had been intent in thrusting it between Lew's shoulder blades but now he was ashamed of his outburst and tried to explain it. "Soggy not assho'e. Soggy rikeab'e guy."

Reed found it hard to contain his laughter and busied himself lighting a cigar before strolling over to Lew. "Buster, you done backed yourself into a corner. It's time you proved up. If you don't make the grade I expect you to drag your worthless hide off Double Square range before mornin'." He turned to a couple buckaroos standing off to one side and instructed, "Put his saddle on Goldy."

A solitary horse bucked out through the sage, kicking dust that hung golden in the setting sun. Lew stayed with it, spurring the big horse until there was no more. He came back and his saddle was shifted to a brown horse named Whiskey and he rode him, too. He did it with such style and enthusiasm that when he returned the buckaroos applauded and even Soggy, apron rippling in the wind, clapped his hands and whistled through his teeth, not for Lew, because he still despised him, but for the genuine horsemanship of the exhibition.

In the morning Orv got his chance on a fair bucking horse and after that was accepted into the elite world of the buckaroo. By suppertime both he and Lew were regulars. They came in to the pleasant aroma of rabbit stew bubbling in the blackened pot slung low over the fire.

After eating, all the men except Lew sat around drinking black coffee; the stars came out and danced in the Milky Way and off in the night the coyotes yipped. One of the buckaroos, a fellow who referred to himself as the Gentleman from Cheyenne, rolled a cigarette, jabbed it into his mouth and reached for a stick from the fire. He had a story to tell and he spoke slowly, drawing the story out.

"'That stew tonight reminded me of a time in Wyoming. I was workin' for a cattle outfit other side of Green River. That's big country. Anyways, one day this stranger comes ridin' in. He's all decked out in brand new, store-bought duds. Of course the cook, like any cook, was anxious to feed him. We talked a bit and the stranger claimed he was a barber by trade but said he was fed up with the business and wanted to be a buckaroo. He had seconds and then thirds of the stew, couldn't seem to get enough. Pretty soon he tells the cook that's the best stew he ever et, wants to know what kind of stew it is.

"'Sonofabitch,' the cook tells him. 'Ain't you ever et it before?'

"'Naw,' said the barber, 'but I sure cut a lot of 'em's hair.'"

With the story concluded there were a few subtle

chuckles. One of the buckaroos got to his feet, took the coffee pot that hung over the fire and began to pour coffee all the way around. When he came to Lew, Lew shook his head no, said he never drank coffee.

The other buckaroos began to tease him, joshing that a man was not a man unless he had an equal amount of coffee and blood in his veins. Reed interceded on Lew's behalf, ''Any man who can ride a bronc like Lew can do what he damn well pleases.'' This brought a murmur of assent. Reed continued, ''Not drinking coffee's no big thing. By the way, he don't touch alcohol, neither.'' And that brought a chorus of jovial kidding from the others.

CHAPTER 10

The fall swing that had taken the chuckwagon and the buckaroos in a big circle on Double Square's thousand square miles of range was complete. Most of the buckaroos were being laid off for the winter, some had already departed. Lew was thinking maybe he and Orv might get their walking papers when Reed called him aside and told him, "Lew, you been a good buckaroo for me. You done everything I asked. But I got a better place for you. Face it, you belong full-time on a bronc. You're a bronc buster, not a buckaroo. I tell you what, I'm goin' to up your salary twenty-five bucks and make you my rough string rider. I don't want a horse to leave this spread that you haven't ridden at least once. Think you can handle it?"

"You bet I can," said Lew. Becoming the rough string rider for the largest horse operation in the country, probably the world, was a dream come true. Now Lew had everything. He would never run out of horses. He would have a bronc for breakfast, one to finish off the day and as many in between as he could squeeze in.

Most days he crawled on the backs of at least forty horses who had never felt the weight of a man before. They were wild mustangs that wanted nothing more than to throw this burden and get back to the open range. Once in a while, on a real snot-thrower, Lew would make a mistake and pay the price by being thrown. But when he picked daisies he would dust himself off and climb back on. One at a time the horses and their tricks were filed away for future reference and Lew became a better bronc rider for the wealth of experience he was gaining.

Each morning Lew rose from his cot and moved about stiffly until the first bronc of the day popped his joints into place and then he could move about freely. The horses consumed Lew and he spent his waking hours in the corral working them. A month went by, two months, three. Winter edged into spring and Lew did not notice Orv was staying away from the ranch, sometimes several days in a row.

And then one day Orv came to the corrals and while Lew was waiting for the wrangler to saddle him another bronc Orv told him, "They offered me the foreman job at Golconda Cattle. I took it!"

"You did what?"

"I took it. I'm the new foreman of Golconda."

Lew, a look of consternation playing across his face, regarded Orv as though he were someone he hardly knew. He could not personally comprehend becoming a foreman of a cattle outfit, could not see why Orv would want to leave a buckaroo job to become a vaquero boss.

"You ever come up short and need a job you always got one with Golconda, long as I'm there."

"I'm a bronc buster."

"Someday you might want to do something else."

The thought was incredible to Lew. Do something else besides riding rough string? And Lew recalled the deal he and Orv had made, that they would work long enough to earn a grubstake and then start running mustangs on their own. Maybe if Lew asked him to reconsider ... no, because he would have to give up his job as rough string rider and he was not ready for that. At Double Square he had everything he wanted or needed; a wrangler to catch and saddle the horses for him and the best bucking broncs in existence. No, he could not turn his back on Double Square until he had had his fill. But someday, he told himself, he would fulfill the dream and chase wild mustangs and then Orv would have a choice to make.

Orv assumed the duties as foreman of the cattle ranch thirty miles away. Six weeks passed before one Sunday morning Lew saddled up and rode to visit Orv. Lately he had been thinking about Orv quite a lot and thoughts of Orv induced the slight rustlings of homesickness for the Wallowa Valley; the majestic blue mountains, the lush grass, the deer and the elk and probably most of all, the evergreens. He found himself actually longing for pine trees, to smell the tang of pine in the air and see the dark green mat of a forest.

Orv had changed his appearance. He was clean shaven. And as he and Lew talked it was apparent that more than physical appearance had been transformed — it went deeper. Several times he mentioned a woman, a school teacher he had met in Battle Mountain, and feebly hinted at the possibility of settling down, starting a family. He came out and said, "I ain't getting any younger."

On the ride back to headquarters Lew felt as though a canyon had opened between himself and Orv, a canyon that would continue to grow until someday it could not be bridged. Surely they would always be friends but Lew could not bring himself to understand the change of attitude and direction.... Why weren't things like they used to be?

For the next two weeks it rained every day, one storm after another and it seemed to have an effect on the broncs Lew rode. The spark was gone; the passion, the zeal was missing and finally Lew decided to take a day off, head in and visit Orv again. On the way he was thinking how great it would be if he could turn the clock back to when he and Orv had first come to Nevada.

Lew reined in; a metal horse shoe crushed a frail white desert lily into the damp earth.

A rider was coming hard toward Lew and when he got close enough Lew recognized the horse as a Roman-nosed gelding belonging to Goconda Cattle Company and the rider as one of the vaqueros, Jim Palmer.

Jim yanked back on the reins and put the horse into a slide that ended beside Lew. Jim was tight-lipped with a grim look to his face. He began straightaway. "I hate like hell to be the fellow that ... that ... brung bad news."

Lew knew instinctively. "Orv! What's happened? Is he hurt?"

Jim painfully expelled a quantity of air. "He's dead."

"Dead!" Lew felt sick to his stomach and dazed. "How did it happen?"

"He drowned. There were four or five of us with him. We were down by the Stone House if you know where that is." Lew nodded. "River can be swift there." Lew visualized the brown swirling waters that would be running high with all the rain. "He was crossing. There was this overhang and when his horse went to get out it gave way and they toppled over backwards." Lew envisioned Orv's face being submerged in the murky water. "I saw him once. He came to the surface. And then we never saw him again."

"You mean you didn't find his body?" Lew was aroused and grasped at a thin shred of hope. "Maybe he's alive!"

Jim dashed the possibility. "Couldn't be. We rode five miles downstream, both sides, didn't see nothin'.

Pat and Tybo went to Battle Mountain after grapple hooks and a boat. I came to get you, figured you'd want to be there.''

''God damn it all to hell,'' said Lew and prodded his horse forward. ''Let's go.''

They dropped out of the foothills toward the valley. Across the way a storm squatted over the Sonoma mountain range and lightning flashed against the flank of Mt. Moses. Lew absently remarked, ''I could understand it better if Orv got hit by lightning and killed. But all the horses he's been on, to have one slip and that kill him. Hard to believe.''

As they approached the river a wagon carrying a small rowboat came down the road from Battle Mountain. Lew and Jim had to cross the flooding Humboldt and down just a bit from where Lew came out he saw a fresh scar where the bank had given way and wondered if that was where Orv had tried to get out.

The wagon pulled in where a group of vaqueros stood around a small fire and Lew, climbing off his horse, spoke to the driver and told him to swing as close as he could to the river. As Lew and a couple of the others slid the boat out the driver made mention of the two boys, a Mexican and a Basque, on the seat beside him. ''Brought these kids 'cause they're lightweight and figured they could grapple.''

When the boat was in the water Lew climbed in and directed the boys to take seats in the stern. Someone dropped a grapple hook tied onto a rawhide lariat in the bottom of the boat. Lew dipped oars and pulled into the surging current of the Humboldt River. He strained on the oars, concentrating his strength to maintain their position while allowing his mind to focus on unimportant details; the roar of the water, the fine mist that hung in the air and muffled the sounds of the squeaking oarlocks, water seeping into the boat from a small crack. He snapped out of his trance in time to bark at the boys as they pulled even with the cutbank, "Throw the hook!"

Both boys helped pull in the grapple, hand over hand until they snagged something and it moved. The Mexican boy excitedly shouted, "We got something."

Lariat coils built and Lew struggled to keep the boat from going with the flood. He watched over the gunnel as the cold muddy water rushed and eddied angrily around the tight braid of the rawhide lariat.

As if in a horrible nightmare a hand emerged, skin blue and not like skin at all, but there could be no doubt it was a hand and Lew's reaction was to groan as though receiving a low blow in a fist fight. He doubled over and the current took control, spinning the small boat, dragging it downstream. Lew pulled on the oars but the strength in his arms and back seemed to have vanished and finally one of the vaqueros tossed a lariat. Lew caught the rope and fastened it to the bow and they were pulled to shore.

After Lew and the boys were safely on the ground the vaqueros hauled Orv in and loaded him face up in the boat and placed the boat in the back of the wagon. Lew took his bedroll off his saddle and tucked it under Orv's head. He mounted and realized how foolish his actions were. The wagon headed toward Winnemucca and Lew rode behind, watching a tiny rivulet of water drip off the end of the tailgate to be swallowed by the sand. He dropped back hurting badly and then tears came and he could do nothing to stop them.

At the funeral home Lew told the director, "Get the body ready for shipment. I'm taking him home, to Wallowa, Oregon. I think that's where he would want to be."

While Lew waited he aimlessly walked back and forth along main street until a pocket watch display in a jewelry store window finally caught his attention. He went inside.

The jeweler handled several watches expounding on their individual merits before carefully removing a goldplated watch. ''This is my finest timepiece, contains twenty-three red rubies and is accurate to within one second a day.''

''What's it cost?'' asked Lew without enthusiasm.

''Seventy-five dollars.''

''I'll take it,'' said Lew, ''and I want 'Winnemucca' etched in it and the year.''

''Yes, sir.''

On the street Lew withdrew his pocket watch, looked at the time and realized the body was probably already loaded on the train. They would be pulling out in fifteen minutes.

He took a seat on the train by the window and as the sagebrush country flowed past he became mesmerized. Time lost all meaning.

''Elgin! End of the line!'' Lew got up and stretched his large frame. He took a couple steps and stopped, trying to put what he should do in order. First, he would have to arrange for a dray to take the casket over the mountains. He could ride with the driver and avoid the expense of renting a horse.

Above Cricket Flat a cloud opened and it rained. Lew cursed, wishing he were riding instead of sitting on the wet buckboard seat.

At the mouth of the canyon, the entrance to the valley, the Wallowa Mountains appeared. They were even more magnificent and majestic than Lew remembered and overcome he turned to the pine box and said, ''Better sit up, Orv, and look around. We're home.''

CHAPTER 11

L ew sat easy in the saddle, flowing with the fluid
movement of the horse as it galloped across the
Nevada high desert. He reined in on the brow of a
windswept ridge. There was not another human within
forty miles of him and he felt his isolation. Perhaps he
had made a mistake in returning to Nevada so soon
after the funeral. He had done it for Orv. He was going
to chase wild mustangs just like they had planned.
Nothing had changed in that regard except Orv would
not be there in person. But he would be in spirit.

A tumbleweed carried by the wind rolled uphill and
Lew found joy in seeing it. Curiously his mind went
back to when as a child he had walked the fenceline of
his parents' homestead turning loose the tumbleweeds
that piled up there.

He sat motionless for quite a long time, the valley
stretched out before him like a large shimmering lake,
remembering Orv and the good times they enjoyed.
Without Orv he was friendless and alone.

And then the self-defeating sorrow passed as the
tumbling tumbleweed had and Lew instinctively knew
what he had to do. "I need a bronc. A high-flyin', snot-
flingin' bronc." He whirled the horse and galloped in
the direction of Winnemucca.

Lew walked into Stockman's, sauntered across the
room toward the bar. This vaquero called, "Sorry to
hear about Orv," and that one, "Good to see you again,
Lew."

Lonnie Colly hollered across the noisy room. "Lew Minor! I been waitin' for you. I got a horse even you can't ride."

The room fell quiet and a big grin spread across Lew's face. "Exactly what I was hopin' to hear." He dug in his pocket, walked the few steps necessary and dropped five twenty-dollar gold pieces on the bar. "A hundred says I can."

The bar emptied of patrons as they followed Lew and Lonnie to the barn below town by the river. Lonnie pointed to a stall. "His name is Helldiver. This is as far as I'm going."

Helldiver was an Indian cayuse with medicine hat markings. Lew approached the stall and Helldiver kicked and struck at the boards. Behind him Lew sensed the jangle of spurs stop. There was a slight trace of alcohol in the air. Without turning he stated in an even tone, "Couple you boys get a rope on this gentle pony. We'll saddle him outside."

Helldiver was brought to the corral and eared down before he could be saddled. No one noticed the door to the barn was left open and with Lew aboard, Helldiver made a sunfishing burst and made straight for the opening.

"The door," yelled someone but it was too late. The door was built low and narrow so a man could lead a horse through but not ride him through. Unless Lew bailed off he would be smashed like an egg thrown against a wall.

Bronc riders, like gunfighters, have reputations to protect. If Lew piled off the news would be all over the country by morning. He was in the saddle to stay. Let the raw-boned horse go to the moon, Lew would be there raking him. At the last possible second Lew ducked and coiled his lanky frame around Helldiver's neck and together they blasted through the opening.

Those spectators perched on the top rail lost sight of the horse and rider but there was no mistaking the level of activity coming from within; Helldiver squealing, dust boiling and Lew whopping, "You dirty son-of-a bitch." And then like a lightning strike Helldiver reappeared in the corraled arena bucking savagely and Lew uncoiled himself from around Helldiver's neck.

Lew and Helldiver were welded; Lew anticipating, reacting in perfect unison with the barbarous moves of the horse. Spurs flashed and sharp rowels cut into horsehide. The battle raged, blood began to ooze from the raking cuts administered by Lew's flailing legs. Little rivulets of crimson stained the white hair. Helldiver bucked until he could buck no more and fell. Lew jumped clear and hit the ground on the run and it was four or five steps before he was under control. Helldiver refused to get up even after Lew gave him a kick to the stomach, a kick as though to say, "Okay, you son-of-a-bitch, I rode you. I'm better than you are. I'm the best there is."

It was not conceit but pride that made him kick the horse and the Lew who had come to Nevada the first time was back. He swaggered when he walked away. Helldiver was left in the dirt, flopped on his side and bleeding. The wounds would heal, unless the flies got to them; they were superficial cuts and nothing more. The real pity of riding such a high-strung animal so far into the ground was it destroyed his innate spirit, the essence of a champion. Robbed of that, Helldiver would most probably spend the rest of his days hitched to a wagon.

Lew, feeling on top of the world, collected his winnings and the crowd dispersed to every bar in town to tell eyewitness accounts, for anyone who would buy them a beer, of the battle fought between Lew and Helldiver.

A vaquero from Pitchfork Ranch, after he heard the story repeated, drawled, "That ain't nothin'. One time down in Lovelock I seen Lew Minor ride the worst bastard I ever seen; and he rode him drinkin' a soda pop. Used a nipple so as it wouldn't break out his teeth. One hell of a ride he put on, I guarantee ya that."

Lew was alone and could still feel the tingle of the lingering effects of adrenalin. And just as the surge of euphoria had washed over him it swept past leaving him dispirited in its wake. He was not happy but told himself he should be. He had made the ride in grand fashion and collected a hundred dollars. What was the matter then? For one thing Orv was not there to pound him on the back and tell him what a wonderful ride it had been. Lew walked past a whorehouse and could smell the whores' French perfume, thought about stopping but kept going to the hotel and straight to his second floor room. He sat watching out the window, the comings and goings of a world that seemed to be passing him by. The difference was Orv. He had been a cheerleader, an ego-booster and above all else, a true friend. Nevada would never be the same without him.

CHAPTER 12

"**I**'ll be, if it ain't Lew Minor. When did you get home? You back to visit or to stay?" asked George Rodgers at the Wallowa livery.

"Not sure," Lew told him. "What's the news?"

"Railroad. That's all anyone talks about. Tracks be reachin' town any day now."

"Guess not much use for a bronc buster, not if the railroad's comin'."

"Might be able to use you the day of the celebration. Bring a long rope. A whole bunch of these folks around here never laid eyes on a train. You might have to rope 'em and drag 'em back." George chucked at his wry sense of humor.

Lew stayed at his folks' place and started making the rounds, looking for a job breaking horses. The day of the celebration, the day the railroad finally reached town, Lew was busy breaking a couple of Ed Robinson's horses to pack. He did not attend even though he could have finished up early had he wanted.

On his next town trip Lew noticed a flyer tacked to the door of the livery advertising the Kit Carson Wild West Show. It would arrive on a special train. The flyer promised, "Stupendous Wild West Extravaganza — Cowboys — Indians." The part that caught Lew's attention was, "Including Windmill — World Famous Bucking Horse. Fifty dollars to any man who can ride him."

The day of the show Lew came early but there was

already a line. While he was waiting to purchase a ticket he overheard one boy tell another, "That there's Lew Minor. He's gonna ride Windmill." The second boy had said, "Bet he don't," and they argued that way as they went to find seats.

Lew climbed the bleacher seats like stairs and sprawled himself over three rows, endured a mock Indian attack and tolerated a gang of make-believe robbers re-enact the Younger gang shootout. He shifted to a more attentive position as a dark bay horse was led to the center of the arena.

"Ladies and Gentlemen! The Kit Carson Wild West Show has the distinct pleasure of presenting to you, Windmill, the finest bucking horse on the face of the earth. Each town we visit we make the same proposition — fifty dollars to any man who can ride Windmill. Before today no man has collected. Perhaps we have a gentleman in the audience who thinks he can ride this horse. If so, let him step forward."

Heads turned and eyes looked at Lew but he stayed where he was, draped nonchalantly in his place.

"Come now. Fifty dollars. There must be one individual who feels man enough to give it a go. Any takers?"

Lew stalled, people were almost to the point of calling his name before he finally accepted the challenge and casually descended the bleachers and hopped over the railing. As his heels struck the dirt the crowd cheered. Many had seen him buck McDonalds' horses down Main Street and stories of some of his most memorable rides in Nevada had found their way up and circulated.

"We do have a contestant." The announcer asked Lew off to the side, "What's your name?"

"Lew Minor."

"This brave young man is Lew Minor." The

applause swelled. "Let's give him a great big hand." It swelled more. He spoke to Lew again. "You from around here I guess."

"Wallowa."

"Ladies and Gentlemen, from right here in Wallowa your own Lew Minor. Say, Lew, is your life insurance paid up? Just joking, just joking. Boys, help him up."

Windmill generally lost his rider with a twisting spin, either left or right, and a reverse counterspin. Lew kept a low center of gravity and knew from experience what Windmill was going to do even before the horse did. The contest was not won on brute strength but on quickness and balance.

"Sir, that was sensational, an eye-popping ride," gushed the announcer who also was show manager. "I would like to offer you employment with the Kit Carson Wild West Show. You would tour with us, be our star attraction."

Lew took the fifty dollars and put it in his pocket. And just that quickly made up his mind.

The crowd greeted the announcement, "The Kit Carson Wild West Show is proud to announce its latest star, Lew Minor," with a rousing cheer of, "Lew! Lew! Lew!"

Lew indeed was the star of the show, billed as the "World's Top Buckaroo"; fifty dollars was offered to anyone bringing in an animal he could not ride.

Every night it was a different town and Lew rode for the win and the show, sometimes riding backwards to the crowd's absolute delight. In Wyoming the horses were mustangs, in Nebraska mules too ill-tempered to work and in Kansas anything and everything.

It was in Eureka, Kansas, another two-bit stop, that

an uncoordinated plow horse fell with Lew and reinjured the same shoulder, his right, that he originally hurt on main street, Wallowa. For a week he could not ride and then when he did his performance was not up to his standards. That night the wild west show train sided and when a westbound freight came chugging past Lew jumped it. He stayed with the train until reaching Roslyn, Washington, where he threw his saddle over one shoulder and duffle over the other and walked up main street. The men he stopped to converse with, almost to a man, were headed into Canada to mine for gold. It seemed to Lew opportunity might be found up north. He drifted that direction; a farmer gave him a ride and lying on a stack of hay as the country passed, Lew was glad to be in the mountains instead of the flat depressing Midwest.

"Sorry, this is as far as I go," apologized the farmer.

"I appreciate the lift," said Lew, grabbing his saddle and duffle. "Could you tell me how far to the next town?"

"Be Okanogan, six miles. Sorry I couldn't take you farther. Sorry I couldn't take you all the way."

Lew, alone on the road, started hiking. A cold Arctic wind blew in his face. He could almost smell the tundra and the ice. It spit snow and he stopped every so often and set his gear on the ground and blew in his hands to warm them.

The last few miles Lew caught a ride with a doctor in his buggy and in town told him to let him off at the blacksmith shop. He went inside, warmed himself at the fire and asked the smithy, "Know anyone needs horses broke?"

"Not comes to mind."

"How about rodeos? Any rodeos going on around here or is it too late in the year?"

"Only rodeo in the whole country is one going on up

to Conconully but you don't want to go up there. That's an Indian rodeo. White man'll never win there." With that he went back to pounding metal.

Lew caught a room for the night and in the morning returned to the blacksmith shop and purchased a horse. It took nearly all his money.

The road to Conconully climbed through narrow valleys and draws and the weather, although the sun did shine, was cool and crisp and there could be no doubt that winter was fast approaching.

Officials at the Indian rodeo demanded ten dollars from Lew as an entrant's fee. Lew did not have it and offered to put up his horse but several Indians who had gathered around wanted him to put up his Lawrence swell-forked saddle. He did.

The bucking horse contest, even the Indian judges had to concede, could go but one way and the championship was awarded to Lew. By the time he left town it was snowing and beginning to stick at that high elevation.

It never occurred to Lew that he was drifting but no one place was strong enough to hold him until winter finally did the trick. A heavy snow trapped him in Chesaw, Washington, only a mile shy of the Canadian border. Lew accepted the seasonal interruption to his wandering and asked around the small town, at the hotel, the harness shop, the blacksmith shop and even the hardware and dry goods store before learning Jack Thorpe was looking for a hired man.

The Thorpe homestead was less than a mile east of town and included scattered outbuildings, a log barn and a two-story house with a steep-pitched tin roof. As Lew rode in there was a tow-headed boy in the barnlot scattering grain to the chickens. Lew approached him and asked, "This the Jack Thorpe place?"

"Yep," replied the seven-year-old. "He's my pa."

Lew dismounted and extended his hand to the boy. "My name's Lew Minor, what's yours partner?"

"Johnny Thorpe. You got business with Pa?"

"Guess I do. Guess I do at that." Lew straightened.

Johnny cupped his mouth with his free hand and hollered toward the barn, "Pa! Man to see you. Pa!"

Presently Jack Thorpe emerged from the barn. He was square-built with gray hair infiltrating a sweeping black mustache. He gave Lew a good looking over as he approached. Lew introduced himself, said he had done a little of everything in his time but most recently had been a bronc buster and was looking for a job to carry him through the winter.

"Any experience driving a stage sled?" asked Jack, still trying to size Lew up. Lew was big enough and had the obvious confidence to tackle most any job but anyone Jack hired would be living with his family and he wanted to be positive, not like the last time.

"Sure, I've had experience with driving sleds. Back in Wallowa that's how you get around in winter. Haven't really ever driven stage, though couldn't be much different."

Johnny had worked his way close to his father and Lew and stood waiting for a decision to be made. Jack sent him away with the admonishment, "Big ears, hadn't you better get back to feeding chickens?" And Jack took a step nearer Lew and in a low voice confided, "If you take the job you have to sleep in the bedroom with Johnny. Some men can't get along with kids. If you're one of them speak up now. The last man Johnny took a pitchfork after, stuck him through the calf. He was a terrible tease, had it coming. I was going to fire him anyway."

The thought of the tow-haired boy ramming a pitchfork into the leg of a grown man, a bully, amused Lew and he laughed. "There won't be any trouble."

"You're hired. You take care of the stock and do the chores and every once in a while I'll have you fill in for me on the stage. I run it up to Rock Creek. That's in Canada. How does that sound?"

"Fine with me."

A tamarack shingle vibrated, worked itself loose and sailed toward Canada on a strong wind that brought with it the threat of warmer air and more snow. The barn moaned and groaned against the assault and tonight Johnny would have been scared if Lew had not been with him. Johnny was afraid in storms like this that a mountain lion come to seek protection in the barn would pounce on him, so he stayed close to Lew while he milked.

"Tell me about Nevada," implored Johnny, trying to ignore shadows cast by the lantern playing in the rafters.

"I've already told you all those stories."

"Tell me again. Tell me about Helldiver," pleaded Johnny, needing a story to keep his mind off mountain lions.

"Well, all right. See, I was running mustangs at the time, went into Winnemucca and happened on this fellow said he had a horse I couldn't ride. I told him I could and the bet was on...." Lew told the story with a dry measured cadence, the howling of the storm adding emphasis; milk squirted into the pail and an elusive change in the sound took place as the pail filled.

Day after day the routine was the same, chores to do and stories to tell; only a few times that winter did Lew get away to drive the stage and even then Johnny, who worshipped Lew and his exciting exploits, rode with him wrapped in the grizzly bear lap blanket to protect him from the cold.

Spring started and stopped at least a dozen times but when it finally broke Lew was able to work a colt outside, going through the training process so that Johnny could learn the basics. A special comradery had developed between Lew and Johnny. Lew was a hero to the boy and the boy was someone who took Lew's mind off moving, searching for the elusive ride of a lifetime.

Lew tapped the colt's shoulder and obediently the colt raised his leg. Johnny wanted to try. His small hand slapped muscle and the colt obeyed. Lew praised Johnny's effort and coached, "That's it, now look at the hoof. See if there are any rocks stuck in the frog or sole. Right here — now even a little pebble like this can cripple a horse, make him go lame. If that would happen in Nevada you're liable to have a mighty long walk. Remember, your horse always comes first. Take care of him and he'll take care of you."

Like a shadow Johnny stuck with Lew; was there while Lew built fence, when he doctored a cow or pulled a calf. Lew enjoyed the adoration, even reveled in it, but as the weather warmed he found himself wanting to leave Chesaw. Maybe he would go on up into Canada for a while, make a swing and drop into Montana. He had heard somewhere that Montana had good bucking horses. Maybe he would give Montana a try.

Jack Thorpe read Lew's restlessness. He valued Lew's hard work and the way he was able to train horses, but most of all he appreciated the patience he exhibited toward his son. Lew was good for the boy, there was no doubt about that, teaching him things about horses that Jack himself did not know. But Jack knew Lew was a drifter and with the warm weather he was apt to move on — unless Jack could provide a challenge to hold his interest.

One night at the supper table Jack passed Lew a piece of rhubarb pie and posed a question he had given a great deal of thought. "Lew, would you be interested in putting on a bucking horse exhibition? Some of the locals have been talking about pulling a fair together and they need a drawing card. I suggested you."

"Sure, he'll do it," injected Johnny with enthusiasm.

Even without Johnny's outburst Lew might have smiled because the idea appealed to him immediately. He shook his head and daydreamed about getting back in the saddle, a horse bucking strong.

Advertisements for the bucking horse exhibition, promising a hundred dollars to anyone bringing a horse that Lew Minor could not ride, were tacked on fence posts along every road in the county.

The exhibition was to be held on ground midway between the Thorpe ranch and the town of Chesaw. The morning of the big event, as Lew saddled his horse, hammering could be heard in the distance as a few extra bleachers were being added at the last minute.

Lew's horse was black, thick-chested and possessed an easy gait that carried it effortlessly across the meadow. A vivid sun burned a hole in the cloudless sky and drops of last night's dew sparkled and threw off a rainbow of color. A quail called from a brushy thicket near the creek. Lew drew a deep breath and for the first time in a long time was aroused and looking forward to the day and the promise of action.

The dark horse entered the freshly plowed arena at a comfortable gallop and swung into a lazy circle. Even at this early hour the grandstand section was beginning to fill. Lew made his first pass and the spectators observed his lanky frame and the natural way he flowed with the movements of the horse. He passed again and they saw his face; long angular nose, high cheek bones and the rangy hollowness of his cheeks. The next pass they focused on more detail; the determined, firm-set jaw, the unwavering gaze of his steely-gray eyes. Around and around he rode and when finally the crowd was in place he put his horse through its riding paces and as a grand finale the horse got down on his knees, with Lew still on his back, and bowed.

The crowd was reserved, clapping politely, until a wild cayuse was led squealing, squalling, kicking and fighting into the arena. This was why they were there, and if it were their animal Lew could not ride, they would be the ones to earn a hundred dollars.

Lew was in the saddle; long legs encased in silver angora chaps drove spurs that bit horseflesh. The rein hand was held high and as the cayuse bucked the other hand waved insolently toward the grandstand.

Johnny, who had had to come with his parents, yelled for everyone to hear, "Look at him ride! Look at him ride!" And the crowd found its voice as throats came alive. It was the passion and the glory that excited them.

Lew rode every horse, thirty-six in all, that day and when it was over he seemed as fresh and ready for action as he did before he started. As the crowd, farmers and miners and wives and children, filed out Lew's attention was throttled by one person in particular, a very pretty girl dressed in a tan riding skirt and a pink, close-fitting blouse. He tipped his hat to her and said, "Good day, Miss. Sure look pretty today." She blushed and went on. Lew hurried to Jack Thorpe and discreetly asked, "That girl. The one with the black hair and slim waist. Who is she? Where does she live?"

"Oh her," said Jack, not trying in the least to hide his grin. "That's one of the Holmes girls, Edna I think. Her folks got a place up there on Pontiac Ridge. Three good-looking girls in the family and the way I hear it you might have to stand in line."

The following Sunday Lew informed Johnny he was going off riding by himself and left, riding hard until he got on Pontiac Ridge. On the hillside overlooking the Holmes place Lew tied his horse to a low branch and sat on a stump. He was there a good hour before the dark-haired girl he had seen the Sunday before emerged. Minutes later the girl was mounted on a sorrel thoroughbred mare, racing for the timber. For another moment he sat watching her tight curls bounce and flow with the breeze; her red blouse sparkling amid the soft green of the meadow and the dark green of the forest. He threw himself into the saddle and caught up to her at the top of the ridge but she reined hard to the left and led him on an exhilarating two-mile chase before she finally stopped, laughing breathlessly.

CHAPTER 13

Bending fiddle strains coursed through the cool Indian summer night as Lew turned the corner and started up the flight of stairs leading to the Chesaw Eagle's dance hall. A group of men were lounging against the rails of the landing, talking in hushed tones and taking turns gulping whiskey. In spite of the moon Lew could identify no one in particular until he was two stairs from the top and a troublemaker named Blondy positioned himself to block the path. He thrust a jug and a challenge at Lew. "Have a drink."

Lew shook his head side to side. Standing as they were it appeared Blondy was several inches taller than Lew. He was much stockier and he was drunk.

"Understand you been seein' quite a bit of Edna," said Blondy and he slurred his words. "Here." This time he touched Lew with the bottle and Lew suppressed an urge to knock it out of his hands.

"I don't drink," he told Blondy firmly.

Blondy took a swig. Lew started to push past but Blondy grabbed him by the arm and threw his worst insult. "I've taken her out and I've had sex with her, too."

Lew grabbed him so quickly, two hands around the neck, that the last word was choked. He bent him backwards over the rail and it seemed Blondy's neck must be breaking. Blondy could not breathe and surely would have died right there had not some of the others pulled Lew away and got Blondy laid out flat.

Lew started down the stairs, methodically, one at a time, boot heels making solid contact with the wood and Blondy, fear streaking his pathetically hoarse voice, moaned, "I never done nothin' with her. Honest."

Lew and Edna were married in a simple ceremony attended by the Holmes and Thorpe families. Lew dressed for the occasion in a white ruffled shirt and black bow tie. Two buttons on an ill-fitting charcoal double-beasted suit coast were buttoned. The only item of dress not borrowed was on his feet, scruffed and unpolished work boots.

At the last minute before Lew and Edna's train departed Chesaw Johnny Thorpe came and gave Lew a hug. When Lew asked why he was crying Johnny said, "It's just I hate to see you go." And he ran away.

The bartender brought a beer and set it in front of Johnny McDonald, bubbles rose to the foamy surface and absently Johnny reached for it, fingers wrapping around the glass, fingerprints magnified. He turned from the window to address the bartender.

"Know what I just seen, Ed?" Johnny said with a degree of smugness to his tone. "Lew Minor has come home and he brung a bride with him."

Ed rocked back in disbelief. "Lew Minor? You don't say. I thought he would roam to the far reaches and always be a bronc buster."

"Me, too. So why the hell did he get married."

Lew, Edna on his arm dressed in a dark blue dress with three-quarter length sleeves and a white belt to define her slim waist, walked past the bar window. Lew glanced in and nodded to Johnny and Ed. They started to wave but the couple had already passed.

Edna paused to read an advertisement tacked to a message board in front of the drug store. It publicized a rodeo to be held that weekend in Grangeville, Idaho. The highlight was the saddle bronc contest with a prize of $75 and a new saddle.

"How far is Grangeville?" Edna asked innocently.

"As the crow flies about fifty miles."

"Why don't you go?"

"Can't cut straight across. There's mountains and canyons and the Snake River." Lew was already toying with the idea. It would feel good to get on a bucking bronc.

"Take the train. That's what it's for. If you went it would give me time to get the house straightened around. I want to make curtains and buy a new rug.... You could win me that seventy-five dollars. You know you could." They walked up the street and Edna ducked into the clothing store and put a new dress on layaway.

Lew took the train to Grangeville, walked uptown and was just reaching for the knob of the hotel door when someone came running down the boardwalk yelling, "They're coming! They're coming!" Lew set his saddle and duffle down, stepped into the street and leaned back against the hitching rail. Five hundred horsemen came barrelling past in the fastest parade on record; they were shouting and shooting and trying to outdo each other. Pedestrians screamed and crowded back into doorways and alleyways like a frightened flock of chickens.

The horsemen raced to the far end of town and pulled up on the sidehill milling around and firing revolvers and whooping. When a hatless gentleman thought it safe he peered out the door of the hotel. The entire street was deserted except for one rangy cowboy leaning against the hitching rail out front rolling a blue-tipped match between his teeth.

Lew noticed something out of the corner of his eye, a man's derby hat, and retrieved it. One horse or a dozen horses had stepped on it, it was hard to tell. Lew looked up and the hatless man stepped cautiously from the doorway. Lew flipped him the flattened hat.

One of the first riders to compete in the Border Days Rodeo celebration was Lew. His draw was an Indian cayuse that bucked disjointedly, stumbled and fell. Lew was thrown, landing in an ungraceful heap on his right shoulder. Pain ripped through him but Lew grit his teeth and got to this feet. He picked up his hat with his left hand, tested the right arm and winced; but as he walked away, back toward the gate, the spectators who were clamoring for a reride could not tell he was hurting.

An official approached. "We're giving you a reride."

A gun fired and Lew turned to detachedly watch the cayuse he had been riding in the throes of death. Her leg had been broken in the fall. They had shot her.

"Guess that's the last buck we get out of that one," remarked the official.

"I'll take the reride now," Lew informed him.

Lew made the ride on a mustard-colored bronc, holding his right arm as close to his body as possible while still making a showy ride. For Lew it was nothing special, an average or a little below average ride, but it was good enough to get him into the finals. He was in the running for the prize money. When he thought of the money he thought of Edna. She expected him to win.

The following day the shoulder was stiff and sore but if he ignored it he would have adequate motion to ride. He won on a horse named Cut-Throat, a wicked spinner and high bucker. No man could have ridden him better than Lew.

The news of Lew's victory in Grangeville reached Wallowa by telephone and Edna was waiting when the train came in. Her first reaction was not to hug him or welcome him home but to turn her palm face up and wait for him to hand her the money.

"Honey, guess what I just heard — the Pendleton Round-Up starts Friday and they're giving $250 first place money and a $350 saddle. Come on, let's hurry, we can wire them your entrant's fee out of this." She flipped through the stack of bills she was clutching. And it was at that point, looking at Lew to gauge his reaction that she saw he was in pain and holding his right arm to his body. "What's wrong?"

CHAPTER 14

L ew rented the last room available anywhere in Pendleton, a hole-in-the-wall above the Silver Spur bar. At one time the square room had been painted aqua green but the color had faded and was now more gray than green and the white casings around the window and door were grimy and smudged with hand prints. There was a wash basin with a pitcher of water on a low marble-topped table, the marble was broken.

Lew glanced around and sat on the edge of a squeaky mattress, scowled at his discomfort, the dull ache in his shoulder. He lay back and arranged the pillow so it took the weight off the arm. That seemed to help. He fell asleep.

Lew awoke to the long shadows of a fading day. The shoulder felt much better and he tested it by rotating his arm, concluded it was more an irritation than an actual injury. Feeling as though he needed to stretch his legs he walked to the Round-Up grounds, ambled across the track kicking at dirt clods. A bull bellowed and Lew squinted into the sun hanging low on the horizon and spotted two men perched on the top rail of the stock pens. He moved in that direction.

The bull bellowed again and the horses ran from one corner of their corral to the other. The two men, Bert Kelley and John Spain, intently watched the horses. They were past Round-Up saddle bronc champions, Kelley in 1910 and Spain in 1911. Spain was first to notice Lew and exclaimed, "Look at the size of that son-of-a-bitch, would ya. Ever see him before?"

"Nope," replied Kelley, "but the way he struts I'll lay twenty bucks he's a bronc buster."

"He's way too tall, no competition. Besides you got the world championship wrapped up, Bert. But if they'd let me compete I'd take it away from you," Spain chided Kelley. "Get a load of the duds — what's he supposed to be — a clown?"

Lew, in no particular hurry, took his time reaching the corrals. He was dressed in a yellow shirt with a bright orange bandana gathered at the throat with a gold wedding ring. He wore Indian beaded wrist gauntlets and a tan cowboy hat shaped buckaroo style with the crown popped up and creased and the brim flat with a bit of a dip in the front and back. The horses spooked again as he came up; he leaned against a post near Kelley and Spain and watched from between rails. Making an attempt at conversation he asked, "How they look to you boys?"

Spain growled, "Probably a hell of a lot more horse there than you can handle."

If it had not been for the injury, Lew told himself he would peel the older man off the fence and roll him in the dirt to teach him a lesson. But at this point he did not want to do anything to jeopardize his chance. The next two days were going to be the most important of his life, riding for the Championship of the World. He started to walk off, changed his mind and turned back to Spain. "I wouldn't bet on it if I was you." This time he walked straight away.

Spain tipped his head in the direction of the retreating figure and told Kelley, "Cocky bastard, ain't he? If that don't beat all."

"Wonder who he is?"

"Don't know, but if he thinks a newcomer can

wander in and win Pendleton he's crazier 'n a pet coon.''

Quarterfinals began in the morning and Lew's draw was Bugs. A small light-colored gelding was led into the arena and Lew approached in a calm, unhurried manner.

He pulled himself into the saddle, the snubbing horse broke away and with the solid assurance of a swinging wrecking ball, Lew assailed Bugs with his spurs and braced himself. Afterwards he could remember very little about the ride, it seemed to him all too routine. Bugs was nothing outstanding but still Lew was judged one of the top ten riders to be advanced to the semi-finals the following day.

Afterward Kelley, who also advanced, said to Spain, ''Well I guess we know who he is now.''

''Nothin' to worry about. You saw the way he milked that ride. Bugs ain't no kind of horse. Let's wait and see what he does with Long Tom or Angel. He'll be pickin' daisies. Hell, Bert, you're right where you wanted to be, on the inside track and as long as you ride clean and don't pull leather you'll win the shootin' match hands down.''

Lew slept soundly and in the morning the familiar sun rose over the humped back of the Blue Mountains in a cascade of colors lighting service berry leaves a brilliant red and clumps of crested wheat grass a summer-dried yellow. He lay unmoving, watching the patterns of slanting sunlight filter through the grime on the window. He pulled back the sheet and as the sun began to warm his naked chest he breathed easily and reminisced about the broncs he had ridden.

He kept coming back to Nevada. Those first days, when he and Orv arrived in Nevada, had been the best of his life. In a way he wished he could go back in time, things were simpler then. And after a few minutes of that type of thinking he recalled he could never go back, was a married man now. He rolled out of bed and got up, extended the arm. The shoulder felt only a little sore and mildly restricted.

Kelley made his ride in the semi-final, a good solid effort, before Lew's turn came on his draw, Butter Creek, a brawny, flaxen-colored horse from Heppner. On the way across the arena Lew went to spit but did not have enough moisture in his mouth and had to settle for merely licking his dry lips.

Lew placed his saddle on Butter Creek and pulled up the slack in the cinch. Butter Creek shied against the snubbing horse. Lew pulled down the stirrup ready to mount, nervousness twisting his stomach until he was in the saddle squirming for a deep seat and at that instant an absolute calm spread over him. He knew what was coming. This horse could not do or try anything he had not seen before. For as long as it bucked, Lew Minor was going to be in control. His pupils dilated a fraction, he was set.

At the periphery of the action Spain poked Kelley in the ribs with an elbow. "Second jump Butter Creek is gonna come 'round, cut back sharp. He'll never last past that."

Once released Butter Creek made two preliminary hops and hooked hard to the inside only to reverse and come back around in a juggernaut move of speed and balance. Lew came out of it whooping and digging spurs asking for more.

"Jesus H. Christ!" exclaimed Spain and it was such an extraordinary ride he found himself clapping. He glanced at Kelley who was not and he stopped.

Before the crowd eleven hundred pounds of horse was melted to a liquid. Lew walked away, holding the injured shoulder as immobile as possible, hurting some but with an expression of contentment. The applause of

25,000 followed him and he felt it run up his spine. He shivered.

Three men were advanced to the finals. First was Art Acord, a rider who always placed near the top, second was Bert Kelley and third was Lew Minor. Acord drew Speedball, Kelley a renowned bucker named Long Tom and Lew got Angel.

It was a point in Kelley's favor when he drew Long Tom. He was assured of a quality ride. Spain had won on Long Tom the year before although his championship had not gone undisputed. In fact, there had been a great deal of controversy. The other two finalists were Jackson Sundown, a Nez Perce Indian, and George Fletcher, a Negro. Sundown bucked off and was disqualified and there were many who believed Spain grabbed leather to keep from being thrown. Fletcher was the only one to ride clean. But it was Spain who won.

The decision, felt by many to be based more on color of skin than riding ability, was booed and Fletcher was mobbed and carried around on the shoulders of the crowd. Later his shirt was cut into small pieces, sold for five dollars apiece and he made more for his non-winning performance than Spain did for winning.

According to Round-Up rules a champion was not allowed to compete the following year. The rule as well as the manner in which he won stuck in Spain's craw and as he idly watched Acord settle himself in the saddle, he longed to be in his place competing. He told himself he deserved it.

On this day neither Acord nor Speedball were of championship caliber. There was no fury in the bucking and no chances taken in the riding. The crowd clapped politely.

While Kelley saddled Long Tom a rodeo cowboy that went by the name Shamrock made it a point to look up

Lew. Shamrock was a young Irishman who had landed in New York a month before and hopped freights cross-country in order to be on hand to participate in the world championship saddle bronc contest. He was a novice with high hopes and his draw in the preliminary round had been Angel. All it took was Angel's looking around and seeing the fluorescent green angora chaps Shamrock wore to go wall-eyed. Shamrock landed on the ground like a fat frog jumping in a pond.

When Shamrock found Lew, on haunches leaning back comfortably against the railing, he said with the heavy brogue of a true Irishman, "Wish I could tell you something about the horse. But it was pretty much a blur, don't you know. Anyway, wanted to warn you, he's got a hell of an opening move."

Lew found himself laughing. Shamrock moved away. The American flags high above the covered bleachers snapped and called attention to themselves. The saddle was being gently placed on Long Tom's back and he danced a bit. From the herky-jerky movements Lew knew Long Tom would be a difficult horse to ride and make it look good.

Long Tom gave the appearance of being awkward. At one time he had been a wheeler on a harvester, until he struck at his owner and shattered his arm. After that he was sold to an Echo rancher who tried to turn the rangy brown gelding into a saddle horse. The first time he crawled on Long Tom he was sent so high he thought he never would come down. But he did, on his head, and was never quite right again. Long Tom had a reputation as an outlaw.

Just before the blindfold came off Long Tom, Spain muttered to himself, "Okay, Bert, don't do anything stupid. Ride safe."

Released from the snubbing horse, Long Tom's head went down. He swung the head left and the rest of the body went right. He tried it to the other side and put some distance in between, popping like a whip. Kelley's green shirt flashed with awkward action but his spurs remained locked against flesh, knees tucked under the protective swell-forks of his saddle. He rode safe and it was a satisfactory ride although nothing fancy. Kelley ran the horse out and dismounted.

The dust enmeshed the sun and Lew sensed a descending layer of unclouded confidence surrounding him. Shadows of horsemen moving about, of Angel being brought to the center of the arena, were long and distorted. All life paused. Lew took several deep breaths, rolled the shoulder and found the gnawing discomfort still there. What did it matter? His time was here. He had the opportunity to prove himself. On this day he could be the best bronc buster in the world. He rolled his neck to loosen the muscles, left fist clenched involuntarily and he pushed himself away from the fence and stood.

Out in the arena three men wrestled with a black gelding. Lew, hat pulled low to shade eyes, scrutinized the behavior and reactions. The horse, his veins showing over leg muscles taut as piano wires, pranced to the building roar of the crowd as Lew calmly moved toward his destiny.

"Show 'em what you're made of!" someone hollered. Lew grinned then, boyishly, and his stride was long and confident. At that point some bronc riders might look to a friend or the crowd for reassurance but Lew had a deadly serious look about him, eyes affixed to Angel. He carried the Lawrence saddle in his left hand and the dragging cinch made a dust trail in the yellow sunlight.

Lew comprehended all the broncs he had straddled up to this point had been nothing but stepping stones to this shot at the world championship. He was ready but he had to wonder about Angel. Could he possibly be, on this particular day, the fiercest bucking horse Lew would ever face? Such an extraordinary challenge sent a chill through Lew's nervous system.

As Lew stepped near he smelled Angel's sweat. He patted and stroked the short black hairs on the throat and allowed the hand to drift over shoulder muscles that jumped and twitched. He was absolutely sure then that Angel was ready. It was now or never and after first stroking the flat back he lay the saddle blanket in place and when Angel was used to it, added the saddle, gently allowing the weight to settle. The cinch was handed to him and he brought it up between the cinch rings in a series of smooth and intricately manipulated loops that could only have been learned through sheer repetition.

Lew stepped back and the fast disappearing sun sent bending rays of buttery light to play on him; silver angora chaps seemed a richer color than they actually were. His blue shirt was bluer than blue. He spoke to Angel. "Take it easy, boy, You're okay. Give me your best. Don't hold back. Go long and hard as you can. Now easy, boy, easy." His hand was out so Angel could smell him. Nostrils quivered and in that instant of distraction Lew took one step sideways, pulled up the last bit of slack in the cinch. He sneered at the annoying pain that shot up his arm to his shoulder. A fleeting thought raced through his mind that if he did fail it would be because of the shoulder.

Left hand reached for the horn while right turned the stirrup out and in a startling fast move he pulled himself into the saddle, sat motionless. Angel shuddered.

"He's up!" came the collective voice of the crowd. To them this would be the highlight of the rodeo. The climax they had come to see. Who was the best saddle bronc rider in the world?

"Let 'er buck!" broke from the crowd in several places at once.

Lew's world had shrunk to a closed sphere around himself and Angel. A voice, not seeming to be his own, told the men, "Turn me loose." The snubbing horse cast away. The cowboy on the blindfold stepped back. Lew snapped a quick look to make sure the mounted judges had not changed positions then focused back to Angel's ears.

The ears flattened with a snap. Solid silver rowels broke the round image of the sun and buried themselves in thick shoulder muscles. There was contact and detonation.

From the grandstand Angel, wild, squealing, farting, appeared to explode in every direction at once; ends swapped, heels kicked a hole in the sky and Lew, with the synchronized rhythm of a pendulum, raked his spurs.

At the zenith of Angel's sunfishing leaps the Indian tepees along the Umatilla River could be seen under his belly. Up in the air, four feet pointed at the last rays of the sun, Angel contorted and all the while Lew was an integral part of the action. Lew and Angel were one. And the ground shook from the plunges and the hysterical cheering and foot stomping of the crowd.

To Lew the violent action moved in slow motion. Bits and pieces, as if snap shots taken by a camera, would be etched forever in his memory: Angel's mane frozen at the top of a buck, the eyes rolled back, the sensations, the wildness and above all else, the feeling of total abandonment. He rode taking chances, he was reckless and stormy.

At the time the savage battle between man and animal seemed to go on without end. And then the pounding wave of the attack crested and the tide ebbed as Angel began to lose strength. The muscles could not replace oxygen as fast as it was being used and wilted. The points of shock were no longer the dramatically underlined jolts they had been.

Angel was reduced to crowhopping, then running and finally called it quits and stood heaving for air in front of the main grandstands. Lew dropped to the ground. His legs, weakened by the exertion, barely held him. His breathing was as forced as Angel's. Without being aware of it he was massaging his right shoulder. He began to feel tingling in his toes and the tips of his fingers. And the last edge of sun dropped below the horizon.

"You the cowboy just won this saddle?" questioned Til Taylor, sheriff of Pendleton and president of the Round-Up. He had been riding the championship saddle on exhibition and was the first to reach Lew.

"Reckon I must be. I'm the only one out here."

PHOTO ALBUM

Jennie, William and Lew Minor (1887)

Lew (1910)

Preceeding page—Wallowa Mountains (photo by Jerry Gildemeister)

Lew Minor at Thorpe Ranch (1912)

Lew and Edna Holmes on their wedding day (April 14, 1912)

Lew at Thorpe Ranch (1912)

Lew and Angel, Pendleton Round-Up (1912, photo by W.S. Bowman)

Round-Up President Til Taylor showing prize saddle for World Saddle Bronc Championship (1912)

Left—unidentified
bronc rider

Above—Bill Mahaffey
on IZ (photo by W.S.
Bowman)

Below—Noah Henry on
Bill McAdoo, Pendleton
Round-Up (1925, photo
by R.R. Doubleday)

Bonnie McCarrol thrown from Silver, Pendleton Round-Up
Wiley Blancett on Corkscrew at the Pendleton Round-Up
(photos by W.S. Bowman)

*Lew and four grizzly
bears he killed in
Alberta, Canada (1920)*

*Lew and Kitty in
beaverskin coats (1925)*

Above—Horse Rex, Kitty and Lew (1924)

Left—Kitty

Below— Lew and Kitty Tennant's wedding day (April 21, 1924)

Lew at Shelby, Montana (1923)

*Lew and friends, Wallowa, Oregon
(circa 1940)*

Lew and Jake Silver after
moose hunt (circa 1972)

Lew at Pendleton Round-Up (circa 1965)

Lew on Polly at Pendleton Round-Up (circa 1965)

Lew at his ranch north of Wallowa (1975)

Lew and Jake Silver at Pendleton Round-Up Hall of Fame Banquet (1977)

Lew Minor with his championship saddle at the Pendleton Round-Up Hall of Fame (1977)

PART TWO

CHAPTER 15

"I'm goin' huntin', see ya later," called Lew. Behind him the screen door slammed, echoing between the house and garage like a lost hound.

Kitty slid open the kitchen window and although Lew was only a few feet away he did not hear its telltale squeak. "Lew, wait!"

"Huh, what's that?" Lew saw her leaning out the window and dismissed her with, "Already said goodbye."

"Honey, wait a minute," implored Kitty. "Radio says a storm's moving this way. Take your raincoat. I'll get it. We don't want you coming down with another cold, now do we?" She ducked inside.

"Ah shit," groused Lew, but glancing at the thick black cloud churning above the Wallowas, he knew from experience it would rain in the valley within the hour and started back.

Kitty met him on the porch, handed him the yellow rain slicker and stole a peck on the cheek before he turned away. She went to the kitchen, started dishwater and one by one absently set the dishes in to soak as she watched Lew walk through crested wheatgrass gone to seed, following the trail toward the barn. Kitty was a small, slender woman who kept herself attractive and young-looking as possible. Her perfume was sweet, but used to excess, and her lips were painted ruby red.

Lew brought a brown mule around and tied it to the hitching rail on the side of the barn. He tried to slip the bit between clenched teeth and when the mule refused to budge, he grabbed the lower jaw, roughly forced the cold metal into place. He disappeared inside the barn and returned carrying the championship saddle he won in Pendleton. The seat, cantle and fenders were well-worn and shiny. He set it on the mule's back and cinched up, pausing for a moment before drawing the last bit of slack to remove his glasses. He squinted in the direction of the house as he wiped at the glass with a handkerchief. He pulled down the stirrup, turned it out and patting the saddle leather allowed himself a moment of nostalgia, fingers tracing over the stamped lettering *World Saddle Bronc Champion.*

"Yep, ol' Angel, you was a good bucker. Ah, yes you was." He congratulated himself, "You rode 'im."

Lew's foot was in the stirrup and both hands on the horn. He pulled, and as he did, the rain slicker rubbed against itself, plastic cracking against plastic. The mule snorted and shied. With maximum effort, Lew kicked his right leg over the cantle and plopped himself in the seat as the mule launched into crow-hopping. Lew's first inclination, his instant reaction, was to rip with his spurs.

Kitty dropped the dish towel and threw hands to her face at the sight of Lew spurring the bucking mule. She ran outside, was part way down the stairs when Lew and the mule parted company. The loose cinch caused the saddle to slip to the side and Lew was helplessly thrown into a barb wire fence. She dashed to where he lay in a heap, rolled him over and cradling his head, began dabbing at the blood on his face with a corner of her apron. It was a deep and frightful gash that ran from his forehead down his nose, across lips and chin.

Lew, coming to his senses, pushed her hand away and struggled to his feet. "That dirty son-of-a-bitch. I ain't been bucked off since I was a kid."

"Honey, we got to get you to a doctor." Kitty was pleading.

"Nope." Lew went after the mule and the blood ran off and spotted the yellow slicker with a sickly orange. He caught the mule, righted the saddle and rode in a circle before telling Kitty, "That's it for this son-of-a-bitch. He's goin' down the road. Now let's get to the doctor."

CHAPTER 16

L ew and Kitty lived at the old Henry Beggs ranch eight miles from Wallowa. Henry, Lew's uncle, had run his automobile into the side of a train and Lew was only heir to the one-story farm house, log barn, garage and 230 acres. Roughly one-third of the land had been cultivated, but Lew used it mainly for pasture, taking off a single cutting of hay a year. The east end of the property reached part way up a timbered draw that led back into scabflats, rock outcroppings, bluffs and deep stretches of woods ending abruptly with a mile plunge into inaccessible Hells Canyon Gorge. The ranch house sat at the throat of this draw, off an oil road that turned to gravel and then dirt and ended at the ghost town of Promise. The lane ran a quarter mile, beginning with a rough cattleguard and punctuated by washboards and chuckholes.

It was the morning of one of Kitty's trips to town. She went once a week for groceries and to socialize, and, as always, she marveled at the mountains and paid little attention to the road, hitting every chuckhole. Tires stuttered over the cattleguard. She turned onto the oil road and lit a cigarette, leaving the stain of her lipstick on the paper.

Ahead and to the left was the neighbors', a ramshackle tar-paper shack. The husband worked the graveyard shift at the mill and was always asleep when Kitty dropped by, as she usually did because it was neighborly, to ask if they needed anything from town.

To her surprise on this day the house looked empty and forlorn. The plastic curtains were gone from the kitchen window, toys that were usually strewn about the yard were missing and a brown oil stain marked where the pickup should have been.

Kitty stopped, opened the car door and as her foot neared the ground a fuzzy gray kitten emerged from where it had darted under the car and began purring and rubbing itself against her ankle. She scooped it up, held it to her bosom and cooed, "You poor devil. I can't believe they would leave you. Why, I can feel your ribs! Oh, darling, I'll bet you're starving. Stay here. I'll run home and be right back."

Kitty returned with a deep bowl and a quart Mason jar of rich cream she had warmed in a pan of water on the stove. Another kitten, this one a coal black, meowed mournfully from his perch on the fence but when Kitty tried to get close, it hissed at her.

On the way home Kitty stopped to leave butcher scraps of meat for the black kitten and took the gray kitten, which she named Smokey, home with her. Smokey received affection and had plenty to eat, spent its days lying in warm sunshine. The black kitten disappeared, never coming to eat the meat scraps or the other offerings that Kitty brought each day for a week. At the end of the week she gave up hope of finding it alive, surmised the coyotes had gotten it and went home, loving Smokey all the more.

Several days passed and Lew was in the barn milking the cow, the door slightly ajar, when the black kitten slipped inside. At first it took tentative steps, but the fragrance of warm milk was sweet on the air and abandoning all caution it made a dash for the cow. Out went a hoof and a ball of fur went flying. Lew turned a teat and squeezed and a few drops of milk landed under the kitten's nose. The kitten went to work licking, following the trail of milk, Another squirt and the kitten moved still closer. Another and it purred.

Lew, in a calming tone he usually reserved for high-strung horses, spoke to the kitten. "Take it easy, boy. How 'bout that. Tastes pretty good, don't it. You bet it does, nice warm milk, You're doin' just fine."

Lew surprised Kitty by carrying his new friend into the house. "Why that's the one from down the road. He wouldn't have nothing to do with me. Where did you find him?"

"I didn't find him, he found me. Hungry as all get out. I give him some milk. Know what I decided to call him? Nig, after Nigger George. Best colored bronc rider I ever saw. Yep, this fella's about as black as ol' Nigger George."

The two brothers, united again, led lives like royalty, getting fresh warm milk from Lew twice a day and begging table scraps and store-bought snacks from Kitty. Their bellies were full and they were content to lie around and grow.

But as the kittens grew into fat sassy cats, out in the barn Polly was rapidly going downhill. Polly was Lew's twenty-seven-year-old saddle horse and her age was all at once catching up with her. Her palomino hide was stretched taut over ribs and her eating was sporadic.

The morning came when he went to check on her and found her unable to rise. Her soft brown eyes were ashamed. She coughed a dry, deep-down miserable hacking cough and had a hard time regaining her breath. Lew, touched by compassion, knew it was his duty to put her out of her misery. He could no longer face her, turned away.

The screen door opening was a signal to the two cats and they swarmed between Lew's legs. Today there would be no milk for them, the calf was already turned in with the cow. Lew proceeded across the front room to the bedroom and the 30.06 leaning in a corner. The rifle was loaded and there was a shell in the chamber. He kept it that way.

On the way out Nig and Smokey cried for milk and again threw themselves at Lew but he ignored them and the screen door slammed shut in their faces. In the barn Lew pulled Polly to her feet and led her down the alleyway. She was unsteady but determined to perform this last act under her own power.

He led her up the timbered ridge and finally, near the upper gate, the arthritic shoulders gave way and Polly collapsed, flopping with an ungraceful groan, head twitching pathetically side to side. Lew chastised himself; he should have taken care of her long ago, but until Polly forced him to take action he had procrastinated, could never pick a day. He bent now to pet her, combing fingers through her mane and bringing a lock of hair between her eyes and straight down her forehead. Ten years ago he had ridden her in the parade at Pendleton and how she had pranced! He had been so proud of her. If fifty, sixty years ago someone had told him his last horse would be a mare, he would have laughed in his face; mares were for raising colts and not for riding. But Polly was different.

"Ah Polly, you was always my favorite, my pet. I'm sorry you had to go and get old. I'm sorry you had to suffer so. Goodbye, ol' Polly."

He unbuckled the halter and stepped away, fastening his concentration elsewhere; to the valley, the dotted fields of baled hay and striped stubble fields, and on to the Wallowas. He remembered Dobbin trail, Polly bringing him down in the middle of the night and boughs slapping his face; the time he and Polly got caught in a snowstorm; the seven-point bull downed with a quick shot from the saddle, Polly hardly flinching. And when he turned to her she was not the lamentable bag of bones but the noble steed of memory. He pointed the rifle, butt firmly tucked against shoulder, cheek in contact with the stock and eye squinting through buckhorn sights. He lined on a point directly behind the base of her ear. The finger began the agonizingly slow process of curling.

The rifle recoiled, Lew's body absorbed the force. Air rushed in to fill the hole created by the bullet's path and sucked in all sound except the echo that rolled on and on, diminishing only slightly with each reverberation.

With this mix of garbled sounds consuming him, Lew started off the hill, shuffling sorrowfully to the barn where he leaned the rifle against the wall and used a manure fork to clean Polly's stall. Afterward he climbed into the hayloft and lay in a depression of hay. Skinny sunrays slanted between logs, dust glinted like super-charged particles, sparrows flitted overhead between rafters. Emotions and memories spun. He thought of his most memorable ride — the year he won the championship. That two minutes and twenty-three seconds was the highlight of his life. It never got any better than that. There was never another horse like Angel. Yep, he sure remembered Angel, undoubtedly the best bucking horse he ever crawled upon. He had it all, that horse — twisting speed, uncanny balance, brute power and above all else, the gallant heart.

"Ah Angel, you was quite a horse," he sighed.

More than a half century had passed since Lew's ride at Pendleton. Not many still lived who had witnessed the spectacle but Lew remembered as if it had happened last week. The color of Bert Kelley's shirt was green. The bronc rider thrown by Angel in the first go-around was Shamrock. He still felt the pride swell in his chest as Til Taylor allowed him to take a victory lap on his palomino. That horse brought him full circle and left him with Polly.

"Lew, where in the world are you? Lew, can you hear me? Dinner's on the table and getting cold. Lew."

"Yeh, I hear. Okay," called Lew and he crawled to the ladder and backed down.

In the days that followed, Lew would catch himself stealing glances toward the sidehill, something within him wanting to see Polly young and frisky, running down the hill, but always there were the turkey vultures making languid circles. It was the fourth or fifth day and he was particularly melancholy. Nig found him sitting on the ground on the shady side of the barn and crawled in his lap. The familiar hands, old but strong, stroked the sensitive spot behind the ears and Nig turned his head to look at Lew. This was the Lew he knew; he had never known the Lew of the past when his body was solid and packed authority. Nig's Lew was thin and worn down.

"Wish you had seen me ride. Ah Nig, I rode with the best of 'em. I sure did. After I won Pendleton I went to Salt Lake Stampede, rode saddle bronc and bulldogged. Made the most money I ever made in my life."

The Salt Lake Stampede was a ten-day show and Lew wanted to add the bulldogging championship to his list of accomplishments. Going into the last day it was Lew and Jim Massey, a world champion from Oklahoma, going neck and neck for the crown.

The steers, out of Wyoming, were big rangy long-horns and given a fifty yard head start before the bull-dogger and hazer were turned loose in pursuit. Lew dropped on his steer late and drove its horn into the ground. The horn broke and Lew and the steer made a somersault. The field man hollered, "Lew, get up and throw 'im." Lew did and for show he held the animal to the ground by biting its nose, his arms raised behind him like a strutting swan. His time was thirty-nine seconds.

As Lew walked from the arena a small bespectacled man came running at him saying he was from the humane society and that Lew was going to pay for hurting the animal. Lew grabbed him by his shirt, held him about a foot off the ground and told him, "I didn't knock a horn off that steer on purpose. Now if that steer had run a horn through me there wouldn't have been a peep out of you." He set him down and commanded, "Now beat it."

Altogether Lew made $1,800 at the Salt Lake Stampede, winning the bulldogging championship but only making day money in saddle bronc because he drew several mounts that were not of championship caliber. After the show he returned to Wallowa and tried to be a husband, earning a living as a meat cutter and sausage maker. The sausage making was Edna's idea; she had the machine delivered and placed in the front window of Lew's butcher shop. Quite often a small crowd gathered on the boardwalk watching Lew Minor make sausage. Lew did not like it, feeling it was demeaning for the world champion to be getting his hands greasy making sausage.

Time for the Pendleton Round-Up rolled around and though Lew could not compete he did ride exhibition, but the most excitement he found that year was not in the arena but in the street. He was crossing the street in downtown Pendleton when a drunk driver almost clipped him. Lew jumped out of the way as the driver lost control and crashed through the display window of Pendleton Drug Store. That was Lew's first encounter with an automobile.

Jim Massey found Lew during the Round-Up and challenged him to a bulldogging contest the next week at Walla Walla Frontier Days. Lew went straight from Pendleton to Walla Walla. He saw no reason to go home.

The first day he was in the money, leading the saddle bronc riding and three seconds behind Massey in bull-dogging. The second go-around Lew's hazer ran over him and when they cut off his boot, bones stuck through the skin.

Lew was completely absorbed in his daydreams of the past. Nig heard the screen door shut, leaped off Lew's lap and went running. Lew was not aware as Kitty slipped up beside him and placed a warm hand on his shoulder.

"Thinking about Polly?" she asked, her concern showing. "You know, Lew, life does go on."

CHAPTER 17

K itty sat in the doctor's waiting room nervously glancing through pictures in *Time*. Out of habit she lit another cigarette and waited for the doctor to call her into his office to tell her the tests' results. She sensed something terribly wrong.

The doctor confirmed, "You have cancer." Kitty's lip quivered but she told herself she was not going to cry, not in public. She refused to look at the doctor, knowing there would be pity in his eyes and she could not deal with pity right now.

"How long do I have?"

"Not long."

"Does my husband have to know?"

"Not if you don't want him to. That's your prerogative. I'm very sorry, Kitty."

"Don't be," said Kitty flippantly. "I've lived a good, full life. Seventy-one years of it." Despite her promise to herself her eyes watered and she removed a tissue from her leather purse and dabbed at her eyes. "I wasn't going to do this."

"That's all right. It's a normal reaction."

"It's just I hate to leave Lew alone."

"I understand," replied the doctor, but there was no way he could.

Winter reluctantly gave way to spring. The robins returned to nest in the apple tree and swallows arrived to flit about the eaves of the house. In the pasture the cows had calves and every morning a doe showed off her twin fawns. Nature renewed itself as each day Kitty died a little more.

One afternoon Kitty felt nauseous and dizzy. She lay on the couch and it helped to focus on the enlarged photograph of Lew riding Angel in his championship ride, hanging on the wall in a simple pine frame. Fervently she wished she had been there that day. Around her a fog drifted and swirled until it seemed as though she were there with the crowd roaring, urging Lew and Angel to their best.

Kitty gently slipped into an unconsciousness from which she would never awaken. So many last minute things were left undone. She had planned at the end to tell Lew goodbye, but was not given the opportunity to do even that.

Lew transported Kitty to St. Joseph's hospital in LaGrande and after the ordeal was over he walked outside, suffering under a sense of absolute and devastating aloneness. When Orv died, at least Lew had mustangs and bucking broncs to distract his mind. Now he had nothing. The white double doors slammed with solid sureness behind him. He stood in the cool of the night looking down on the sleeping town. Somewhere near the river a pickup truck was downshifted and backfired and an eastbound freight gave a solitary warning at a crossing.

Lew had been forsaken and self pity welled in him because he was eighty-six years old with few living friends and no family at all. He told himself he could die right now and it would make no difference to anyone. The unfairness of it all seemed to overwhelm him and he began beating fists against the brick hospital wall, flailing away, an old man striking out in sheer desperation. The knuckles were cut and bleeding, but there was no pain because the pain inside was so great.

Lew pulled into the garage at home, got out and stood beside Kitty's car, deciding he would sell the car and get it out of there. He moved toward the house a defeated man, took a seat in his recliner, leaned back and raised the foot rest. The mantle clock marked the seconds and struck on the hours, the electric refrigerator would come on sporadically, hum for a few minutes and shut off. At one point Lew asked the stars, "Why did she leave me?"

There was no definition to hours, days, weeks; cycles of going to the bathroom and feeding the animals simply repeated themselves. Most often Lew lapsed into thoughts of Double Square, Kit Carson's Wild West Show, Headlight, Helldiver.... Without Kitty he had nothing to tie him to the present. He was adrift on a sea of meaningless time.

Little by little he became consumed by his own inactivity and grief. At the bottom of this emotional sinkhole he concentrated on his failures in life and not the euphoric peaks. Most assuredly his biggest mistake was marrying Edna. It had been a disaster from the beginning. They clashed like bolts of lightning.

It was Edna who had pushed him into the butcher shop and Edna who tied him to a home and strangled his freedom to go where the four winds blew and the horses bucked best.

Their relationship reached a dangerous climax when he was confined to bed after the accident in Walla Walla. They tore at each other like alley cats and when Lew could get on his feet he left her and did not stop running until reaching Nanton, Alberta.

He crawled off the Canadian Pacific and crossed from the depot to the Nanton Hotel, moving with a definite limp. He was carrying his saddle and apparently the fellow leaning back in a chair with his feet on the hitching rail read the lettering because he came down on all fours and pushed back his hat.

"Where you from?" he demanded to know.

"Oregon."

"You win that saddle or steal it?"

Lew did not reply. He flung the hotel door open and entered. He was at the desk signing for a room when the fellow from outside followed him in. He remarked straightforwardly, "So you're the world champion."

Lew looked him in the eye. "Yep."

"One question. Don't get mad. But I seen the way you was limping and ... well, I was wondering ... are you crippled?"

Lew gave a snort. "Of course not. I can ride."

The man beamed, extended his hand. "That's what I wanted to know. Excuse me for being so rude. My name is Dave Ragain. Welcome to Nanton."

Lew looked at Ragain's extended hand and made no effort to shake it. Ragain withdrew it and tried to cover his embarrassment, "So you're a professional bronc rider. Ever found a horse you couldn't stay with?"

"Never." A smile of confidence crossed Lew's face.

Ragain snapped to attention. "Have I got a deal for you. We can both make money. Six miles down the line is Stavely, you came through it, and tonight's the big baseball game between Stavely and Nanton. Be a hell of a crowd. A fellow name of Orr has a horse in Stavely never's been rode. The deal is I cover the bets, you make the ride and we split down the middle. Fair enough?"

Lew thought for a moment, eyed Ragain and decided he was greedy but probably not dishonest. He would keep an eye on him. "Sounds fine to me."

As soon as the baseball game concluded and before

the crowd could disperse, Orr brought his unridden horse onto the playing field. It was a chestnut mare with flaxen mane and tail named J. J. Lew stood off to one side and was amused at the small size of the horse. He expected something big and rawboned, smiled confidently, knowing it would not be much of a contest. Ragain took all bets and signaled for Lew. As Lew approached, the limp was hardly noticeable.

Lew made riding J. J. look easy. He took his share of the winnings and used it to make a down payment on a quarter section of land, sight unseen, in a valley thirty miles west of Nanton. He was told there was a cabin on the property and he figured to winter there, bought grub and was about to leave town when Edna caught up with him. They had a long talk and reluctantly Lew agreed to take her to the cabin. The next morning they left Nanton on horseback, leading two pack horses along a muddy and rutted road. The scenery was spectacular with fresh snow in the Rocky Mountains, the foothills rich with golden poplar, bright red willows and the dark green fir trees. They passed moose, elk and deer grazing in the open.

Breaking over a rolling divide they saw their new home. Happy Valley was a narrow, oblong valley running parallel to the craggy peaks of the northern Rockies. Lew told himself that these mountains were even more grand than the Wallowas, at least they were taller.

The cabin was situated with a window facing the snow-capped, rock-strewn peaks. Beside it was a log barn filled with hay, a good set of corrals and twenty-seven head of bred cows.

Happy Valley was remote and there were few other settlers. Most were renegades or eccentrics at best. One of them, a big red-headed Irishman named Tom DeVinney, would hike to Nanton every Friday no matter the weather, to catch the train to Calgary where he sparred with prize fighters. Another, John Chaffin, had posed for Charlie Russell's picture *Rope a Grizzly Bear*. Lew was warned by one of his neighbors, "Keep a close eye on your cattle or else two-legged wolves are likely to run 'em off." Happy Valley was a notorious haven for cattle thieves, an ideal holding area for cattle stolen on the plains. From Happy Valley they were trailed through Crowsnest Pass into British Columbia and on down to the northwestern United States.

Lew quickly acquired the reputation as a top notch horseman and neighbors brought their troublesome horses to Lew who gladly topped them off. Mart Armstrong brought Lew Old Mart, a knothead prone to crazy antics when the mood hit him. Old Mart had been through fences, into rivers and down shale slides in his checkered career. He had the type of personality that would never allow him to buck first thing in the morning like a decent rebel, but sometime during the day when the rider least expected it, Old Mart would cut loose.

Lew was working those tendencies from Old Mart. He rode him into the mountains and was skirting around the top of a thousand-foot cliff when Old Mart went into his antics, rearing, staggering, bucking when he could. Lew gave a quick look to judge the distance, timed himself with the motion of the animal and when it was evident Old Mart was going to buck over the edge, Lew piled off and hit the ground with arms and legs outstretched, fingers and toes digging in. Behind him in space was a frightened whinny that never stopped. Lew counted "thousand-one, thousand-two, thousand-three" and the sickening pop of flesh striking rock wafted up the rock wall.

Lew hiked to the base expecting to find his saddle smashed, but Old Mart had belly flopped over a boulder and the Hamley saddle, except for a torn cinch and a few nicks and scratches, was good as new.

That first winter Lew and Edna lived hand to mouth, surviving on wild game Lew shot. In the closed environment of a snowbound cabin their strong personalities did battle. It was war. And when the weather broke Lew moved out, camping on the forest reserve and occasionally visiting Nanton and other area towns to trade cattle and find a bucking horse to crawl on. He won money riding and was a shrewd trader of livestock. By summer he had increased the herd size to 350 cows.

With fall approaching Lew hired a couple drifters, George Hillock and Walter Brandon, to help him round up his cattle and bring them off the forest reserve. He never would have hired Hillock had he known Hillock had been a Mountie at one time but recently was arrested for stealing cattle. Rumors later guessed Hillock avoided jail by promising to break the cattle rustling ring known to operate out of Happy Valley.

With Hillock and Brandon's help, Lew made a sweep of the reserve and in the process they picked up nearly 200 head belonging to Harry Streeter. Back at the corrals they separated the cattle and Lew told the hired men to drive Streeter's the five miles through the hills to his place.

Hillock and Brandon, who slept in a tent near the Minor cabin, arrived home late that night. They spotted a lantern shining through the cracks in the barn and when they peered in they saw Lew skinning a cow. From what Hillock and Brandon could see they thought it was a roan cow.

The following day Hillock visited Streeter and asked if there was a chance he might be missing a roan cow. Streeter told him, "Hard to tell until the strays come in. Even then it's rare we get everything."

"I witnessed Lew Minor butchering one of your roan

cows. It had your brand on it, a Walking O on her left hip. Walter Brandon saw it, too."

Lew was arrested and charged with cattle rustling. At the trial Hillock and Brandon testified, swore under oath they witnessed Lew butcher a cow carrying Harry Streeter's brand. Edna attended the trial but instead of sitting on the defense side of the courtroom she sat behind Hillock and Brandon.

Lew took the stand in his own defense. Judge E. P. NcNeil asked him several questions. "Mr. Minor, did you have a quantity of money when you came to Canada?"

"No, sir," Lew told him honestly, "just the clothes on my back, and my saddle and gear."

"How then, in a relatively short period of time, have you been able to purchase a ranch and run three hundred and fifty head?"

"Well, sir, you see, I rodeo around some on the side. I won three hundred bucks in July at Medicine Hat. I'm a bronc rider and maybe I shouldn't say this but I pick up money on bets now and then. I get around quite a bit. I'll tell you one thing, I never come by a dishonest dollar in my life."

The judge refused to believe Lew, found him guilty and imposed sentence, a choice of five years easy time or eighteen months hard labor. Lew chose hard labor.

Like falling down a rat hole, the arrest, trial and sentencing occurred so smoothly, in spite of neighbors who vouched for Lew's character and honesty, that it was speculated the system had been greased to teach others in Happy Valley a lesson.

Lew found himself the victim, legs bound in irons and hands cuffed behind his back, being led up the steps to the Alberta provincial prison in Lethbridge. Behind locked doors the jailer read the sentence to be served. The leg irons and cuffs were removed and Lew was led downstairs. Voices droned from the cells, it was dark and the acrid smell of rotting life permeated the air. Lew was ordered to strip and shower and then was marched along a hallway to a green room where he was fitted with green coveralls and a button-down shirt of the same color.

A civilian behind the counter made an inventory of Lew's clothes and possessions. He double-checked everything on the list, even opened the pocket watch to make sure there were insides. When he did, Lew could read the inscription "Winnemucca 1907" and see the time was a quarter past two.

"Sign here," the man directed, "when you're released you'll get everything back."

In the open holding facilities there were three tiers of cells, thirty-four cells per level. Lew was assigned number 57. The jailer led the way up the iron steps to the gangway for the second tier. Lew's cubicle was no different from the others, a rectangle ten feet by five with a bunk along the wall and a basin in the corner. Cold unyielding concrete separated adjoining cells with bars blocking the front.

Lew was in company with the most desperate and feared criminals in the Province of Alberta. He sat on his bunk and listened to their voices and as the sun went down the voices twisted around themselves, becoming birdlike chatter at the end of a day.

Locking Lew behind bars was tantamount to snubbing a wild stallion. He was overwhelmed by the emotions of captivity. His basic instinct, like the wild horse, was to run, to get away, But now he was trapped. The walls began to squeeze in on him until he found it difficult to breath. He closed his eyes but that made it worse. Finally he had to grab hold of the bars and hang on. Downstairs in the locked basket the Winnemucca watch ran down, stopped at half past nine.

Lethbridge Provincial Gaol was a self-sufficient prison and inmates were assigned work depending on past employment and experience. Lew was sent to the mule division. He watered and fed and made sure the mules were properly shod and fit to work. He tried to tell himself he could have done worse, that he could have been placed in the fields or as a cook's helper but it was little consolation. The mules were a poor substitute for bucking horses.

While he was incarcerated, Lew had time to think. He knew he did not want anything more to do with Edna, had heard she was pregnant with Hillock's child. The ranch in Happy Valley he wanted nothing to do with, either. All he wanted was his freedom, freedom to drift, to always be on the lookout for a horse that would measure up to Angel. Maybe horses like that no longer existed. It was obvious the automobile was replacing horses. The time was fast approaching when it would be tough to give a horse away.

Lew endured eighteen horrible months of confinement and the same jailer who had locked the doors, unlocked them. Lew traded in his green prison uniform for his own clothes and began to feel better when he scrunched the cowboy hat on his head. He gave forth with a loud sigh and inhaled freedom. He wound the Winnemucca watch and time began again.

The Hamley championship saddle and his gear had been stored at a friend's house and Lew picked it up, purchased a horse and rode. Which direction he went was immaterial. It happened to be south. All he wanted was to put miles under the saddle.

It was the end of December, bitter cold with a wind swirling the snow, but weather made little difference. After eighteen months of confinement Lew rode through the night. When he reached the little settlement of Milk River he stopped to warm himself and ask about employment on one of the ranches in the area. There was nothing available he was told.

The following evening was New Year's Eve, the temperature skidded to fifty below zero and rather than risk riding, Lew laid over. He went to the New Year's dance and stepped out of the howling wind and blowing snow into a dance hall filled with warmth and friendly people who knew nothing of his past, neither that he was an ex-convict nor that he had been world saddle bronc champion.

A pretty girl dressed in knickers and a bulky white sweater smiled at him and he asked her to dance. There was something about her, some immediate attraction and though he told himself to avoid this girl, he kept asking her to dance and before morning he was helplessly in love with Kitty Tennant.

"Kitty! Kitty! Kitty!" Lew awoke calling her name. While he had slept and dreamed, the Big Dipper spun around the North Star. His muscles were stiff and his left ankle sore. He was cold and alone, Nig had slipped outside to hunt for mice. He sat there in his easy chair without any incentive to get up and face the day. Kitty was gone.

CHAPTER 18

L ew was yesterday's hero; there was no place for him in the modern world. His youth, strength, ambition and bronc-busting genius had succumbed to the passing of time. No matter. Storms still attacked the Wallowas each winter and the summer sun came to shrivel the wildflowers.

The hour Kitty died, Lew quit living. Smokey ran off and never returned. Lew sat, did nothing and that winter he even lacked the resolve to start a fire because it would have to be replenished every few hours and he did not want to be bound to a schedule. It was all he could manage to do chores and as it was he sometimes forgot the chickens.

Winter's final blizzard blew itself out and warmer air replaced the cold. The sun broke through the cloud mass and glared with dazzling strength off the snow and into the house. Lew got up from his chair with the thought of getting a blanket to cover the window, but instead he stepped onto the porch, realized how warm it was and went for a walk below the house to where the creek cut back and forth across the snowdrifts. It was near the water, in warm soil, that Lew discovered a buttercup. The cold, snow and lack of sun had all worked against the small burst of yellow but yet there it was. Lew picked it and felt the softness of the petals with his fingertips, then discarded the little flower on the blanket of snow. He returned to the house, resumed his seat in the leather-covered chair, sighed, dozed, awoke, moaned because of the pains of a lifetime and dozed again. He dreamed he died.

When he awoke he continued to remain motionless except for an occasional batting of an eyelid, thinking what it would be like if he were to die. If it were not for the heart thumping in his chest and the clock announcing the hours, he might think himself dead. What bothered him was not the dying, but what would happen to him afterwards. How many weeks would it be before his body was found? What would he look like, maybe just a skeleton. And someone had to feed Nig and throw a couple bales of hay in for the cattle and ....

It became obvious he had to do something and eventually it came to him. He went to the garage, started his pickup, had trouble engaging the clutch and ground gears as he tried to slip it out of neutral and into reverse. He finally managed and then it was the same thing to get it stopped and into second. It was the left ankle, the one shattered at Frontier Days, that bothered him and it was not until he was on the oil road that he was able to successfully shift from second to third and another quarter mile before he found high.

Lew pushed open the door to Silver's Market and stepped in, bringing the biting stench of burned clutch with him. On the way to town he had been unable to remove his foot from the pedal.

Jake Silver, a square-built man with a crew cut, a hunter and fisherman when he was not minding the store, waved his hand in front of his face to blow away the smell and remarked, "What's on fire?" He was twenty-five years Lew's junior, had known Lew all his life and could tell from the smell that Lew had been riding the clutch again. "Can I get something for you?" he asked.

"I come to talk to you," Lew told him.

"So shoot," replied Jake, observing Lew closely

now. In the past months, since he lost Kitty, Lew had really gone downhill. He had lost weight and needed a shave, his dentures no longer fit and his normal ruddy complexion had paled. Jake figured Lew wanted to talk about his health, wished instead they could be swapping stories about bear hunting.

Jake was aware of Lew's Adam's apple bobbing up and down as a preliminary to talking. "Jake, I've had dealings with you over a lot of years and you've always been honest." Lew removed his Stetson, fingering the brim as if it were either painful for him to broach the upcoming subject or hard to find just the right words. He shrugged and began.

"Nobody cares about wild broncs no more. Guess it don't matter. I'm an old man, Jake. I outlived my usefulness. Since Kitty left me I been thinkin' what it'd be like if I got down and couldn't get back up. I'm afraid nobody'd find me.

"I got a proposition for you. If you'd look in on me every week or so, make sure I'm still kickin', when I do go I'll leave everythin' to you; pickup, ranch, my saddle, lock, stock and barrel. Got no kin to leave it to anyway. What ya think?"

Jake was caught off guard by the request. After all, hadn't he grown up with the legend of Lew Minor? He had heard and repeated every story there was; never thought it would come down to this — him looking out for Lew Minor — and now he stalled.

"Let me talk it over with Verna. Her and I would have to discuss something like this but I think we can work something out. I'll tell you right now, though, that if I do it it won't be for the inheritance. Hell, Lew, you might just outlive me."

"I hope not."

123

A few days later Jake drove to Lew's ranch and told him, "Verna and I talked it over. She said she didn't mind if I was to keep an eye on you. So I guess from now on I'll come out every week or so. I'll call ahead, though, and if you need anything I'll bring it."

"Thanks, Jake," Lew pumped Jake's hand. "You don't know what a relief it is to me. Only one thing, I want to be buried beside Kitty. Did you know the cemetery is only three miles from where I was born? I went a lot of places in this ol' life to end up so close to where I come in. Suppose you're too young to remember, way it used to be, everybody ridin' horseback."

Jake sat on the upholstered rocker, Kitty's chair, and asked, "Remember the time you ran cattle up near Troy and Al Victor and I brought you that spoiled bay gelding? You used those big Spanish rowel spurs."

"You bet. What ever happened to him? How did he do for you after that?"

"He wasn't a bucker no more, but you took all that snap out of him and he wasn't good for nothin' after that."

"Well," drawled Lew, "that's a spoiled horse for you. Those things do happen."

Every Saturday Jake made the trip from Wallowa to Lew's ranch. But one week Jake was busy at the service station-convenience market that carried his name. Sunday morning he started up the Promise road to visit Lew and on the S corner at the school house he overtook Lew's blue pickup. He followed, gravely displeased at the way Lew drove, careening from one gravel shoulder to the other, brake lights on all the time. Lew never even saw Jake behind him.

When Kitty was alive Lew used to always honk his

horn twice as he pulled into the garage, the old habit dictated he honk this time and as a result he was late in hitting the brakes, the pickup went too far, struck the studs at the far end and the garage shuddered. Lew crawled out and walked through the open end and was surprised to see Jake there leaning against the fender of his car.

"I'm okay. You can go." Lew was curt, then softened somewhat, "Thanks for coming."

Jake thought perhaps he should apologize for not being there the day before, decided against it and opened the car door and slid behind the wheel. He sat a moment without starting the engine, watching Lew hobble across the drive toward the gate. He moved slowly, swinging the left leg because of the bad ankle. Jake saw an old man against the backdrop of a drab fence missing pickets here and there and a house in desperate need of paint. Jake wished he had the time and money to fix things, thought Lew deserved better.

Lew pushed on the gate, gave up trying to shut it and climbed the steps and went inside. As Jake backed around he noticed Lew's face peering from the kitchen window.

That evening Jake told his wife Verna, "I sure don't like to see Lew driving. His eyesight ain't what it used to be, his hearing's going bad, he can't take his foot off the pedals and he swerves all over the road. I'd hate for him to hit some kid on a bike or for that matter he could just as easy meet a log truck head on."

"Not much you can do about it," offered Verna and Jake admitted she was right.

Melting into the darkness Nig approached the porch, leaped to the sill of the window with the broken screen and balanced there before dropping to the floor. He placed a dead field mouse on the threshold and squeezed through the door that had been left slightly ajar for him. With mincing steps he crossed the room and sprang onto Lew's lap so gently that Lew did not awaken. The mechanical cadence of the mantle clock filled the dark void of the room. Once or twice Lew snored a bit, the clock struck hours and time moved on.

The mantle clock, a hump-shaped battered thing, had been brought over the Oregon Trail by Lew's mother. Inside a narrow drawer on the clock's base was a newspaper article from the day Abraham Lincoln was assassinated. When the clock chimed five times, an hour that was off by several hours, Lew raised his eyelids. Greeting him the sun shone through leaves on the cottonwood tree and fell in a dappled pattern on the photograph of himself on Angel. The sight of it inspired him to stand. He felt good this morning knowing it was Saturday. He stepped over the dead mouse without ever seeing it and through the clutter that had become the front porch. Outside a meadowlark sitting on a post of the picket fence twilled a melody. She flew away when Lew opened the door.

Several steers grazed in the meadow pasture and Lew leaned on the fence watching them, musing he had to do something with them. It was long past when they should have gone to market. He wandered over to the barn and fed the chickens. The chickens had been Kitty's and that was why Lew kept them. They were allowed to roam free and managed to fend for themselves in the warm months, chasing down grasshoppers and other bugs, and having to rely on Lew's sporadic feeding when it was cold.

"Well, there you are," interrupted Jake. "Didn't you hear me honking?"

Lew stood grinning at Jake, happy to see him. They

sat on a bale of hay in front of the log barn enjoying the morning sunshine. Overhead two red-tailed hawks circled, from time to time they screeched. Jake made general conversation for a while before telling Lew the news.

"Jim Blakeley was in the store the other day. You know he's about to turn a hundred? Anyway, he says he's going to ride in the Round-Up parade and he wanted me to ask you and see if you would want to ride with him."

"Jesus Christ, he's a hundred. Hell, he was only a couple years older 'n me. Well, I guess that's about right. He was the sheriff in Wallowa when I come back from winnin' Pendleton. I'll never forget what he said, he said, 'You're the world champion and no one can ever take that away from you.' You know, Jake, God damned if he wasn't right. Yep. He was right.

"I guess it would be pretty good, couple old farts like us ridin' side by side but only thing is I don't have a horse. Maybe I could pick me up a horse. Ought to be able to find somethin' if I looked around. Yes sir, I'll just bet I could. Tell you what, next time you see Jim tell him by God yes I'll ride with him in the parade."

Lew bought a horse from a neighbor and started riding it every day. The horse was a palomino, looked similar to Polly and Lew called her Polly. She was gentle and steady, a good horse for him and for the first time in a long time Lew showed enthusiasm. He was up early caring for Polly, currying her and graining her. The horse gave him a purpose and the thought of riding in the Round-Up parade provided direction.

Lew was making a sashay in the pasture when he saw Jake's car turn down the lane. He brought Polly into an easy gallop and headed for the gate.

"You're riding real good," complimented Jake as he climbed from the car.

"Oh no I ain't. I'm sloppy as hell. My knees don't work like they used to and I'm all over the saddle."

Jake kicked at a rock, refusing to look at Lew. "Lew, I hate to say this, after you've worked so hard and all, but Jim Blakeley's granddaughter put the kibosh on things. She thinks it's too dangerous for him to ride in the parade. He had his heart set on it, wanted to be the oldest cowboy there, and I know you wanted to be there, too. Guess it's not in the cards. He wanted me to tell you. Pretty much broke his heart not going."

"Shit," mumbled Lew and again he was an old man. For a few weeks he had been different but now the defeat was back inside and he felt sorry for himself and sorry for poor old Jim Blakeley.

CHAPTER 19

It had been seventy years since Lew won his first rodeo competition at the Wallowa County rodeo and in commemoration he was asked to be grand marshal of Chief Joseph Days celebration. He took his Hamley saddle from the tack room and carried it into the house where he saddle-soaped the leather and polished the silver. Fingers found the scratches and scrapes of a lifetime and he recalled the incidents that caused them; Old Mart going over the cliff, the time in Medicine Hat when the bronc bucked into the fence, but for all the use, the Hamley saddle was in remarkably good shape, strong as the day it was crafted by J.J. Hamley.

Lew did his evening chores, fed the chickens and grained the new Polly. He would ride her in the parade the next day and he petted her and told her how good she looked. He even gave her an extra flake of hay. Polly acted nervous, pawing the floor of the stall. Lew looked around, saw nothing that could be upsetting her and returned to the house.

In the barn a thin column of white smoke curled toward the peak of the roof where it collected in an ever thickening pool. Internal combustion sparked the fire and flames became evident. Polly was in a frenzy, rearing and falling, throwing herself against the stall rails.

The kitchen window was open but Lew did not hear Polly's wild squeals, did not smell the smoke which charged the swirling air currents with its pungent odor.

Mice began evacuating the barn. The crickets were strangely quiet sensing the impending doom but Lew never did, sitting in his chair facing the Wallowa Mountains outlined in black against the fading sky.

Down in the valley a farmer stepped outside for a quick look at a calf that he had pulled that afternoon. He was the first to spot the fire, by now a reddish glow that invaded the darkness, and called the fire department.

Lew noticed the flashing red light on the pumper truck and the long line of headlights coming down Promise road and was surprised when they turned down his lane. He pushed his glasses further up the bridge of his nose, sat up and watched them come over the cattle guard like a long snake, headlights dancing crazily.

It was only then that he became aware of the shimmering illumination emanating from the barn and he rushed for the door. A four-wheel drive pickup slid to a stop in front of the gate. The driver hopped out, a bottle of Olympia in hand. Lew tried to get past him but the fellow grabbed him by the shoulder and held him back. "Nothin' you can do 'cept watch it burn."

Lew pulled away, went nearer the flames until the heat was like the Nevada summer sun on his face. He was to blame, he knew it and the shame burned more fiercely than the flames. If he could smell, if he could hear, if he could see, if, if, if ... and God damn he detested being so decrepitly old. He hated himself and the barn roof collapsed sending a shower of sparks shooting into the black of the night.

Jake found Lew, told him how sorry he was. Lew wiped at an eye, perhaps he had been crying but it was hard to tell.

"You know, Jake, I've had thousands of horses in my life but I swear to God, this is it. I don't want no more.

I'm just too damn old to take care of 'em.''

"Jake, you there?" spoke Lew so loudly Jake had to tilt the telephone receiver away from his ear. Verna, in the other room, could hear and wanted to know, "Is everything all right?"

"Lew, you all right?"

"Jake, I called 'cause I ain't ready to give 'er up, not yet, I want to kill me another elk 'fore I hang it up. I done borrowed a horse, that big bay of Beemers, and I'm goin' hunting. No sense you comin' out tomorrow."

"When will you be back?" Jake wanted to know.

"What's that?"

"When will you be back?"

"Sunday. Yep, that's right, Sunday."

After Jake placed the receiver in the cradle he hesitated for a moment and Verna, reading his mind, told him, "No way you can, Jake. You know how busy you are opening day."

"I know, but Lew's just too old to go off like that all alone."

"I know you're concerned but you can't babysit him. Lew is going to do what Lew is going to do."

"You're right, but I'd feel better if I was with him."

Lew headed the bay horse up the ridge away from the ranch. At the top he paused, turned in the saddle and picked out the landmark mountains: Mt. Howard, named after the cavalry officer who ran down Chief Joseph and his band; Aneroid; Matterhorn. Behind those he visualized rock-faced China Cap, Eagle Cap and Flagstaff Butte where he had killed a seven-point bull elk. He remembered switchback trails, jewel-like lakes and the profusion of alpine wildflowers, reds and blues with occasional yellow and white mixed in. Like viewing a photograph he pictured himself above Minam Canyon, so far above that the river was a soundless, wandering thin white line. He told himself, "Sure I might get older and my body might go to hell but the mountains will never change," and that somehow reassured him.

He exhaled and the chilly air fogged his breath. The horse, anxious to get going, pawed the ground and Lew gave it its head. Behind the saddle a bag containing a tarp, a sleeping bag and essential cooking gear bounced with rolling movement. Lew kept one hand on the saddle horn. He never used to touch the horn except as a casual, cocky gesture when he would rest a hand, a wrist or forearm, but now he gripped the horn to maintain a tenuous balance.

Lew made camp that afternoon in a timbered swale beside a creek that gurgled over granite rock flecked with sparkling mica. He warmed a can of pork and beans, had to eat it with his knife because he had forgotten a spoon. He set the tarp in tent fashion and crawled in his sleeping bag when it got dark.

In the morning there were several inches of snow on the ground, making ideal hunting conditions. He saddled the horse and rode only a mile from camp before locating tracks of a single elk. He followed the trail as the elk browsed on moss and when Lew caught up he cautiously dismounted, slipped the rifle from the scabbard and tied the horse to a low branch. He took a position behind a boulder, used it as a rest, pointed the rifle at the brownness of the elk, an easy target with the backdrop of white. The snow muffled the rifle report but for several seconds the echoes bounced around Wildcat Canyon. The spike elk's legs buckled and he went down but almost as quickly he was on his feet again and charging into a lodgepole thicket.

Lew pulled out his Winnemucca watch to check the

time. He would give the bull a full half hour and probably it would lie down and stiffen. Otherwise, if he kept hot on the trail, the bull might run five miles. While he waited he checked on the horse and got himself a pocketful of shells. He would have to go into the thicket on foot and when the half hour was up he hunched over and started following the low-tunneled game trail. The thicket closed around him, the only light being from holes in the canopy where the snow had sifted through, snow that was spotted with blood.

Lew nearly tripped on the elk draped over a windblow, eyes glazed and tongue hanging out. A blue grouse, feathers ruffled against the cold, sat nearby, intently watching and when it felt threatened it rose in a whirr of motion, startling Lew because he had been admiring his elk.

Out in the open fat snowflakes were falling but Lew was unaware; in the dim light of the thicket he sliced open the elk's belly and began pulling at the warm guts. Later, when washing his hands with snow he discovered he had slashed his left wrist, a serious cut that had nicked the artery. Blood pumped to the surface and he watched detachedly because he felt no pain. To slow the loss of blood he made a patch with elkhide, laying the fleshy side to his own, then cut a long thin strip of hide that he used as rope to bind the patch in place. When he pulled on the knot to tighten it his false teeth came loose. He searched in the snow but could not find them.

A sharp biting wind full of snow began to howl and the trees moaned and swayed. Lew started back for his horse but the cold seemed to have settled in his left ankle. He had difficulty walking and had to use the rifle as a crutch. His plan was to ride out, bring help back to remove his elk.

"By God, you did it, you got your elk," he mumbled

to himself and tugged at the scarf he wore to protect his chin and mouth from the rawness of the wind. The snow was blowing into drifts when he reached the spot where he thought he had tied the horse — the horse was nowhere in sight.

"Piss on you. Find your own way home, you jug-headed son-of-a-bitch, and ya better not rub off my saddle." The wind tore at his words. He stood brooding, knowing full well his predicament and longing for the comfort of his chair at home. It crossed his mind to sit down, let the cold take over and die, but that thought passed and he staggered forward, dragging his left foot. The snow continued, distorting his sense of direction and strong-willed determination was all that kept him going.

Late that afternoon Bill Young, a self-described hermit of the woods, stepped to his porch for an armload of wood and found Lew, obviously in trouble. Bill brought him inside, put him in a chair beside the fire. Lew was in bad shape. He had lost his glasses and his skin was turning blue. He was freezing, exhausted and disoriented. The only reason he had made it was because he was such a fighter. Bill warmed a small pan of water on the stove and fixed a hot toddy which he forced Lew to drink. It revived Lew and he began to shiver and finally he spoke, "I got myself in a hell of a fix. Killed a spike. My horse run off. I cut myself, got lost...."

"Take it easy," cautioned Bill, "now just take it easy. You're all right. I'll fix ya up with a fresh bandage, you take it easy and first thing in the morning we'll find that elk."

Jake, anxious to check on Lew, went out to the ranch about the time everyone else in town was headed to church. Lew was not around but he did find the horse standing by the gate, wanting to get through and go home where he would get something to eat. Jake knew Lew had to be in trouble but being of the old school of thought that a horse always came first, he pulled the saddle and was moving in the direction of the house to telephone the sheriff when he heard a pickup roaring off the ridge, bouncing over rocks covered with a few inches of snow.

Bill and Lew were in the front and the spike elk in the back, Lew all smiles. He gave Jake a one-armed hug and told him, "Ya should've been there. By God, ninety years old and I got my elk. Not many men can brag about somethin' like that."

After surviving the elk hunting ordeal Lew's attitude was improved and his body responded. Pain he endured every waking hour did not bother him as much. He busied himself doctoring cows, shoveling manure from the barn and that spring when the weather improved, he rebuilt a section of fence.

Elk season rolled around again „but Lew had no intention of hunting until he spotted two cow elk in the pasture. He decided on a whim, since it was going to be so easy, he would kill another elk. He got his rifle and worked himself into position for a shot.

Unbeknown to Lew, two LaGrande hunters were sitting on a rimrock outcropping watching the elk with field glasses. They saw one elk flinch and then break into wild flight. A second shot rumbled between hills and the second elk fell. Binoculars followed the first elk. She ran a quarter mile, tried to leap a fence, collapsed and draped herself over the barb wire.

Lew gutted the elk he knew he had killed, dragged it with his pickup to the garage where he used a block and tackle to hang it. The LaGrande hunters watched all this and on the way home they stopped at Crawford Oveson's ranch and told him what they had witnessed.

Crawford paid Jake a visit. "You and I both know Lew doesn't have a cow tag. Now I don't mind a man hunting if he uses the meat. But what I can't understand is why Lew would shoot two cows and only take one. He could go to jail. You better talk to him."

Jake confronted Lew and Lew lied, denied shooting and said it had to be someone else. "When did it happen?"

"Yesterday afternoon."

"Well, I thought I heard a shot but you know my hearing...."

"Goddammit, you're not telling the truth. Just tell me why did you kill two elk and leave one?"

"All right, I admit I killed a cow. She's hangin' in the garage but I sure as hell didn't kill two. Who said that?"

"Two hunters were watching through binoculars. They told Crawford Oveson and he told me. The second elk is hung on the fence by the upper gate."

"The hell you say."

Jake tried to reason with Lew without hurting his feelings. He would have liked to say, "You're too damned old to hunt. You're a danger to yourself and everyone else in the woods," but instead he suggested that he and Lew plan one special hunt and then Lew, for once and for all, should call it quits. "You always tell me about Canada — how good the hunting was. What say we plan a moose hunt in the Canadian Rockies? Just you and me. We could go to your old stomping grounds and you could show me around."

"We could leave right now," proposed Lew. "Say, did I ever tell you about the time I killed four grizzly bears?"

"Yes you have but I wouldn't mind hearing about it

again.''

"By God, that's where we'll go, up around Mt. Rae country. Good huntin' there. Well I tell ya, it was fall of the year, about the time bears start thinkin' about hibernatin' and ...."

CHAPTER 20

Jake's faded red Jeep pickup ground uphill following a curvy highway flanked by service berry bushes and willow trees. The lay of the land jogged Lew's memory and he pointed to a grassy flat. "I been here. Used to be a set of corrals and a barn right there. Me and Kitty, when we was comin' to Wallowa from Montana, we camped here. We trailed everything we owned; had maybe twenty-five head of horses, a cow and a calf, couple lambs, six turkeys.

"Weren't fences in those days, drove everything cross-country. I had me a good dog, border collie named Sparkplug and he kept the stock lined out and moving. He'd even work the turkeys. He was a great ol' dog. This one time a woman came out and threatened to call the sheriff, said we ruined her garden but I don't think we did. Another time we come through a town and a bunch of kids ran up when we stopped and asked if they could carry water for the stock. They thought we were a road show and wanted free tickets."

The Jeep rumbled along. They crossed the border and continued into the Milk River country and Lew took an active interest, pointing out various landmarks and telling stories. But finally he began to tire, involuntarily his head bowed and he slept.

When Lew first came to Canada he was in his prime and he pictured himself that way in his dreams. He was not the man with bones brittle as chalk and joints and old injuries aching, a distortion of his former self, thirty pounds under weight, muscles atrophied and skin a bloodless color. He endured and his body betrayed him.

Lew was asleep, slumped in the seat, jaw slack and head resting on the window. Jake was driving. It was night and the headlights cut a well-defined tunnel through the darkness as they traveled down a gravel road. Ahead was a sign reading "Chilaco Ranch" with an arrow pointing off to the right. Jake turned that way.

Chilaco Ranch was situated in the heart of moose country, thirty thousand acres of woods and sloughs connected by slow moving channels. As Jake pulled to a stop in front of the headquarters, a two-story log cabin, Lew awoke. The cook was washing supper's dishes and when Lew and Jake wandered in he directed them, "Store your gear in the bunkhouse. The guides should be around in a bit to introduce themselves."

Lew had brought along his Hamley saddle thinking there might be a chance for him to ride. He dropped it on the floor beside his bunk as two Indians walked in. The shortest of the two was wearing a mackinaw and had a stocking cap pulled low, almost hiding his eyes. He directed a question to the visitors, "Which one Jake? Which one Lew?"

Lew and Jake identified themselves and the shorter Indian said, "I George Shell. I guide Jake." The other Indian introduced himself as Tony Petel. He asked Lew, "Where get saddle? You ride 'm bucking horse?"

Lew threw back his shoulders and bragged, "I won the world championship."

"You have family?" Tony wanted to know.

"Well, I was married, couple times."

"Have children?"

"Naw." Lew shook his head side to side.

"Maybe rode 'm too many bucking horse." Tony and George laughed a private laugh between the two of them.

There was no need for Lew's bringing the saddle because in the morning after a hearty breakfast Tony and George readied two aluminum flat-bottomed boats. They started Mercury outboard motors and with Lew and Jake in place in the bows they pushed off into a dense, muddy fog held close to the water. Within a few feet the dock had disappeared.

Lew stared straight ahead, seeing nothing; thoughts of Canada and of Kitty swirled around in the close environment. He loved Kitty, he missed her now and wished she had had the opportunity to see the country of her birth one last time. Her face was vivid and he remembered how she looked that day he proposed, so radiant and alive. He had told her about Edna and the eighteen months he spent in prison and still she wanted him, had thrown her arms around him and whispered she loved him and yes she would marry him.

On the way up, coming through Lethbridge, Lew had seen the provincial jail out the window of the Jeep. He had wished he could have had those stolen eighteen months back and that he could be big and strong as he had been then. But it was a dream.

The sun burned its way through the fog and the two boats followed a broad slow-moving channel. The Rocky Mountains were impressively outlined with a dusting of fresh snow.

George and Jake were several hundred yards in the lead and it was Jake who spotted a bull moose feeding in a slough off the main channel. George cut the engine, leaving only a slight trail of oily smoke to mark the path.

Jake made a perfect shot, placing a bullet behind the front shoulder and his tag was filled. Lew spent the next three days and seven shots before he finally connected. The meat was cooled in the ranch's big walk-in cooler and the next morning they wrapped the quarters in tarpaulins, loaded them in the back of the Jeep and started south. Lew, hollow-eyed and face drawn, slept a good share of the way.

At home Lew fell into a familiar abyss of preoccupation, tipped back in his recliner with his feet up. More often than not Nig would be lounging on his lap. The mantle clock methodically noted the passage of time. Lew could hear the faint chimes but not the ticking. There was a low, boiling roar that filled his head. It was always there, even if he awoke in the middle of the night.

It was Saturday and Jake was knocking on the door. He finally had to let himself in, went over to where Lew was sitting and told him, "I was afraid something happened. I've been trying to call. Why didn't you answer?"

"What's that, Jake? Speak slower, 'n louder." Lew was drooling. He must have felt it because he took a swipe at his chin with the back of his hand. "I can't seem to hear none too good."

"The phone. I've been trying to call."

"That damn phone, ought to just have 'em take it out."

Jake told Verna something was going to have to be done about Lew's hearing. The next day Verna made an appointment for Lew with an ear specialist in LaGrande.

Lew told the doctor, "I can't hear worth a damn. Guess I knocked around too much when I was young but she's been a pretty good ol' life, yes she has."

The doctor cleaned Lew's ears and ran a series of tests. On the way home Lew told Jake about the doctor's treatment. "He filled my head with water, jabbed an ice pick in my ear and dug out a bunch of wax. Don't make me hear one bit better.''

The hearing aids arrived and Jake made a special trip to LaGrande and back to Lew's ranch to deliver them. Lew did not have much to say as Jake fit them on his ears. "I still don't hear nothin'," he told Jake and started fiddling with the volume control until the delicate instrument emitted a high-pitched, piercing shriek which made Lew wince in pain. He pulled the hearing aids from his ears, telling Jake, "I'll try 'em a little later," and lay them on the end table.

"You know, Jake, the worst part of gettin' old ... I used to ride street carnivals and rodeos but nowadays people can't imagine. I think about the horses I been on and I wonder how I ever lived so damn long."

Once a month Verna cooked something special and Lew was invited for dinner. Those meals gave Lew a burst of nutriment because he made no effort to maintain a balanced diet. On his own he ate those foods which were easy to fix, easy to chew and that would slide through his system.

One Sunday they were having fried chicken, mashed potatoes, gravy, and green peas. That was Lew's favorite meal but when he did not eat, Verna asked, "What's wrong, Lew?"

"I don't know. Nothin' tastes good anymore. Everythin' tastes the same. I got no taste, she's played out on me. I'm gettin' too damn old."

On one of his visits Lew was particularly fascinated by Jake and Verna's new color television. He thoroughly enjoyed watching it and it prompted Jake to quietly suggest to Verna, "Maybe if Lew had a television of his own he wouldn't spend so much time thinking about the past, maybe he wouldn't be so lonely."

"Why don't you get him one for his birthday?"

Jake carried a package in and gave it to Lew. He tore away the paper and grinned when he saw it was a portable color television. He thanked Jake, pumped his hand ardently and said for him to thank Verna, too.

On his next visit Jake found Lew sitting in front of the screen, sound turned off and the color adjusted to show only blue and red in overpowering extreme. Jake tried to adjust the color but Lew stopped him. "Leave it alone. That's the way I can see it best." When Jake asked him his favorite show Lew responded, "That fellow makes music with an accordian. I like to watch the dancin' girls."

CHAPTER 21

Wallowa Valley neighbors have a way of knowing each other's business. Someone told the preacher at the Christian Church that Lew was failing fast. The preacher decided to pay him a visit. He knocked on the screen door but there was no answer so he stepped inside the porch to the house door which stood slightly ajar. Nig surprised him, blasting between his feet and up and through the torn screen to the outside. It was at that point he caught his first whiff of gas, stepped closer to the door and the smell was much stronger. He looked through the opening and could see Lew in his recliner. Knowing that old people sometimes commit suicide with gas, the preacher threw open the door and rushed in. He was moving in the direction of the propane stove to turn it off when the refrigerator kicked on.

The explosion blew the oven door off its hinges, broke several kitchen windows and scooted the preacher along the floor on his rear like a snowball traveling on hot glass.

Lew awoke in time to see his would-be savior down on all fours scrambling through the doorway. Later the preacher called Jake and Jake went out and fixed the windows but there was nothing he could do to repair the oven door. Lew told him that was all right, he never used the oven anyway.

Another visitor, having heard Lew's condition was rapidly deteriorating, arrived. He was a real estate salesman and Lew was confused about the man's intentions, thinking he was there to listen to stories.

"Yep, I won 'er all. See this picture here? What's it say?"

"It says," began the salesman, having to stand to read the writing, "'World Saddle Bronc Champion, Pendleton, 1912'. That's nice. I came to talk about something else. You have a real attractive acreage here. I'm sure I could find a buyer if you would like to place it on the market."

"Palouse?" questioned Lew, not hearing what had been said. "Sure I been up in the Palouse. Used to be a few wild mustangs running around in them hills. Now they got 'er pretty well planted to wheat."

"No. No. I didn't say Palouse, I said place it on the market. I said I could sell your ranch for you."

"Sell my ranch. Hell, it don't belong to me. I'm leavin' it to Jake. He deserves it. He's taken care of me. I've seen it all, yes sir. Used to work for Double Square, rode rough string. They was the biggest horse outfit in the country, ran ten thousand head...."

The salesman was exasperated. "I'm sorry, Mr. Minor." He looked at his watch. "I would love to listen but I'm already late for an appointment. Maybe I'll stop back. Goodbye and thanks for your time."

Afterward Lew thought how nice it was of the fellow to stop. He guessed he was still a celebrity.

A low-slung Chevy with chrome rims and baby moons limped uneasily over the cattle guard and moved deliberately up the lane dodging chuckholes. Several times it bottomed out, its frame grinding against a high rock. Lew saw the rig coming, figured it was a pheasant hunter.

"Hello, Mr. Minor. My name is Eric and this is Jim," stated the Eastern Oregon State College student. He was probably twenty-one or twenty-two but looked nineteen. There was a flare-up of acne on his forehead and he was wearing sandals and white socks. He was about to say something more but Lew seized the right hand that was extended and pulled Eric uncomfortably close. Eric could smell his bad breath as he focused on several long hairs that grew from Lew's nose. Lew, in a loud voice, demanded to know, "What's your name?"

Eric disengaged his hand from Lew's and took a step back. He began again, pointing to himself and then Jim. "ERIC. JIM. WE ARE WRITING A THESIS ABOUT COWBOYS FOR SCHOOL. WE WANT TO INTERVIEW YOU. TAKE YOUR PICTURE."

Lew caught one word. "Cowboys! We never were cowboys. If you ran cattle you was a buckaroo, or vaquero, that came from the Mexicans. I was a bronc buster. Yes sir, by God, and a good one."

"I WANTED TO ASK YOU ABOUT...."

"I'll be right back," stated Lew, dismissing himself and going into another room. While he was gone Eric looked around, noticing the garbage in the kitchen that needed to be taken out, dirty dishes, a pile of soiled clothes on the floor by the bedroom door and the dominating stench of urine. For some time Lew had had trouble at night controlling his bladder and therefore very often wet the bed. Jim noticed the general untidiness to the house but it was the enlarged photograph on the wall that captured his attention. His hobby was photography and he hoped to make it his vocation. He studied the black and white print realizing it was quite old and reflected on the scope of photographic advances. He wished it were a color print.

146

Eric came over and whispered, "Wonder if that's him," referring to the photograph. That shocked Jim who had not connected the young rider on the fierce bucking bronc with the old man he had seen.

Lew appeared in the doorway dressed in an outrageous moth-eaten full-length beaver coat and a flat-brimmed, buckaroo-shaped Stetson hat pulled low. Lew stood hands on hips, jaw thrust defiantly forward and the boys were not sure if this was a joke and they were supposed to laugh.

"My wife Kitty, she was from Montana. We lived in a cabin on the bank of Teton River and winters it was sixty below. I fed cattle for Daniels brothers. Spare time ran a trap line, caught enough beavers, thirty-two, so Kitty and I could both have coats."

Lew advanced across the room and took a seat in his chair. "One time I was checkin' the trap line. Had a trap set on the far side of the river. Only way to it was crossin' on a beaver dam. Sure enough that particular day I had me a big fellow so I whacked him up alongside the head with a stick I carried for the purpose. But see, when I did I done lost my footin' and fell in the beaver pond. Christ Almighty, was it cold. I walked straight home but it was so cold that before I got there my clothes froze stiffer 'n the pecker on a stud horse."

Lew stood and removed the coat, handed it to Eric who was amazed at its weight, estimating it was twenty or twenty-five pounds. "PRETTY HEAVY."

"Naw. Only wear it when it got real cold. Fifty below it don't weigh nothin' at all."

A tag inside stated the coat had been made in Great Falls, Montana. The fur was still delicately smooth except in the moth-eaten bald patches. Eric pulled the coat on and flipped up the wide fur-lined collar that once protected Lew from the biting cold wind that blew off the Rockies. He fumbled to button the oblong bone buttons. On him the coat looked ridiculous. Because he was short the tail that hit mid-calf on Lew drug the floor. He squirmed out of it and handed it back to Lew. Eric and Jim sat on opposite ends of the couch. Over their heads was the photograph of Lew and Angel.

"WE WANT TO KNOW ABOUT RODEOS. THE LAST RODEO YOU WERE IN, WHAT WAS IT?"

"Last rodeo ... my last rodeo?"

Eric nodded enthusiastically.

"Last rodeo would been Shelby, Montana, just before we moved here to Wallowa. Would of been '27. Same time as the Dempsey-Gibbons heavyweight championship. Gibbons and I was friends. I knew him personal. We palled around together. He was the one asked me to put on a rodeo. I told Kitty afterwards, I said, 'That's it for me. No more rodeos,' and by God I never did go back."

"WHAT HAPPENED AT SHELBY?"

"Oh, little accident. See, I was puttin' on a bulldogging exhibition, was a little late droppin' and ended up goin' face first into the sheep wire. Had sixty-some stitches. Afterward Gibbons told me I looked like a peeled potato. Still got scars. Look, right here on my forehead and my neck. Damn near cut my throat, I did. When she gets really cold, lip here'll quiver and I can't stop it. Don't bother me, though, not like the shoulder and ankle. They hurt all the time. Ache sort of, don't ya know.

"When I was your age I was bigger and stronger 'n both you put together. Now I feel every bump and bruise I ever got and I got hundreds, no thousands, millions.

"Yep, got my start breakin' cavalry horses and there were some buckin' broncs in those days." Eric began to take notes on a yellow legal pad and Jim shot pictures. "One day in Wallowa I rode a hundred and five horses in one day. Yep. Hell, I guess I probably seen it all. I seen too damn much."

"MR. MINOR, YOU HAVE LIVED FROM THE AGE OF HORSEBACK TO THE SPACE AGE. HOW DOES THAT MAKE YOU FEEL?"

"I was born the other side of the hill there, in a log cabin ... what was that?"

"SPACE AGE — MAN WALKING ON THE MOON."

"Ah hell, I don't believe that. If they did, tell me what would hold 'em up there. Naw, hell, they never done that."

Eric smiled for want of anything better to do. It surprised him that Lew should not believe. He had been reared in the space age and took satellites, astronauts and moon landings for granted.

Lew dug through a pile of magazines beside his chair before locating the copy he wanted of *Frontier West*. He showed Eric and Jim a story about himself and while Eric read the story, taking notes, Lew rambled about horses he had ridden in Nevada. When Lew began repeating himself Eric stood and insisted they had to get back to the dorm for dinner.

After they had gone Nig returned and jumped on Lew's lap; he stroked Nig and Nig purred.

"Wake up! Wake up!" Jake was shaking Lew awake. "You were sleeping awful hard."

"Oh, Jake. How are ya?"

"I'm fine. What were you doing, dreaming? Dreaming about a gal or something?"

"Hell no. When a man hits his nineties he don't think about women no more. I was just rememberin' when Orv and me went to Nevada. Boy, those was the days. Nevada, ah Nevada. Sometimes it seems so clear and all, just like it was real. Swear to God. Just like it was real."

"What got you thinking about Nevada?"

"Couple kids came around, from over to the normal school in LaGrande. Wanted me to tell them about bronc bustin'."

"You know," mused Jake, "I've never been to Nevada."

"Ah Jake, you ought to go see it, big ol' sagebrush flats and mountain ranges. Mustangs. Hell, mustangs all over the place. A fellow could make some money roundin' 'em up."

Jake was thinking aloud. "I wouldn't mind visiting Nevada some time. One of these days I'll have to do that."

"Won't see it any younger," insisted Lew, and then an idea presented itself. "You got a new rig. Me and you could run down and be back in a week. You're a good driver, Jake. I sure would like to see ol' Nevada again. Yes I would. Boy, would I."

"Suppose that would be a good way to break in the car. Besides I've been looking for an excuse to get away. I'll talk it over with Verna."

Verna thought it would be more practical to postpone the trip until cooler weather that fall but she did not object when Jake said Lew might not last until fall. He said it was something he wanted to do for Lew.

The car was loaded and ready to go Saturday evening and before dawn Sunday morning Jake and Lew headed for Nevada. It was noon when they dropped into Vale and the full impact of the desert heat became evident. The blinking temperature light on the bank read 97 degrees and the heat drained Lew's energy. They followed a narrow valley where the Malheur River twisted and rambled, the muddy current guarded by willows; farmers baled hay, cattle grazed on irrigated pasture. Lew fell asleep.

On Drinkingwater grade the new Chrysler overheated, lost power and Jake coasted to the side of the road. A cloud of steam enveloped them. Jake looked around for water but the landscape was barren; he stood surveying the desert landscape waiting for the car to cool and the sun to sink farther into the Drinking-water Mountains.

Lew slept though it all. Finally they got going again, limping to the summit. Lew awoke momentarily and Jake was not sure if he had even seen the yellow sun's orb balanced on the fifth mountain range over. Lew mumbled something unintelligible and slept.

"You've been dead to the world for the last four hours." Jake had the car door open and the motel room key in his hand. "We're in Juntura. How does a nice cool shower and clean sheets strike you?"

They spent the night in Juntura but were up early in the morning hoping to get a jump on the day and avoid the hot afternoon sun. They turned south following a gravel road that wound around through hump-backed sagebrush hills. At one point a band of antelope ran alongside and Jake clocked them at 45 miles per hour before the animals broke into a slight depression on the flat plain and disappeared. They came out on the highway at Crane, once an important town at the terminus of the railroad but now just another wind-blown spot on the map. From there the road was smooth blacktop and they sped south.

Across an endless sagebrush valley another road could be seen a great distance away veering off to the right and when eventually they bisected it Jake read "White Horse Ranch" lettered on a fifty-five gallon drum which served as a mailbox. Lew must have recognized the general lay of the land or perhaps caught a glimpse of the lettering.

"Where are we?"

"Said White Horse Ranch."

"Hold 'er a minute." Jake began to slow and pull toward the shoulder. "I used to know a vaquero from White Horse name of Billy Parker. Hell of a good fellow. One time we run into each other in a goddamn blizzard. Two days we rode together, tails into the wind, across the Alvord and into the Sheepshead Mountains. Yep, ended up pretty good friends, yes we did. Think there's any chance he could still be alive? He was about my age. Sure would like to see ol' Billy one last time."

"If you want we'll go," exclaimed Jake. He headed the Chrysler back the way they had come and at the intersection turned left; within seconds a rolling cloud of dust boiled behind.

After twenty miles on a dirt road they came to White Horse Ranch, an oasis of green poplar trees in a gray sea of sagebrush and sand. The manager of the ranch came out as Jake and Lew exited the Chrysler and asked, "What can I do for you boys?"

"Tell ya what I'm looking for, an ol' friend of mine, Billy Parker."

"Funny you mention the name," stated the manager. "I was thinking about him just the other day. I never knew him but my dad used to tell stories about Billy Parker, real colorful character. Got killed what, forty or fifty years ago, a gun fight in a dispute over a spring."

Lew had stepped close and had his head cocked so his right ear, his best, was closest to the manager's mouth. The manager spoke slowly and deliberately. "Story I remember best was the time Billy and a dozen other vaqueros drove a thousand head from Island Ranch to Winnemucca. They was coming into the stockyard when some bright engineer started ringing his bell and the cattle...."

"Stampeded right through the middle of town," interrupted Lew. "And it took us until after dark to pull 'em out of the alleys and backyards. Afterwards Billy brought out a bottle and 'fore long those vaqueros had their minds set to get the bell. Did, too, stole it off the engine, took it back to Island Ranch and I suspect the cook's still usin' it. Last I heard he was."

"Yep, Billy Parker, he was really something," chuckled the manager. "But he's been dead and gone a long, long time. I know where the grave is, no marker or anything, just out there in the middle of the desert. I could show it to you if you wanted to ...."

"I don't think so." Lew was shaking his head side to side.

Jake and Lew continued on and in the shimmering heat sun devils were born and raced across the flat desert, disappearing as the sun began to sink toward a distant range of mountains. There was a sign ahead and Jake read it aloud, "Paradise Valley."

Lew sat up straight in the seat and looked around, exclaiming, "That's my old stompin' ground. Hey, I know what we could do. We could swing up that way and catch a room at the hotel. It's a nice, clean place. Maybe in the morning we could have a look at Double Square headquarters. I'd give anythin' to see her once more."

Twice along the route to the town of Paradise Valley the Chrysler struck rabbits and when they hit the undercage Lew turned questioningly to Jake who mouthed the word, "Rabbit."

Paradise Valley, weathered buildings under giant cottonwood and black willow trees, did not look right even from a distance and as they came closer Jake realized what it was; there were no cars, no people, no life. The town was a ghost town. They stopped in front of an empty false-fronted building. Up and down the street other vacant buildings faced each other and there was an awkward moaning of wind blowing through them.

"Won't be staying here tonight. Going to be dark 'fore very long, better get on in to Winnemucca." Jake stated, but then relented and turned the ignition off. "Guess as long as we're here you might as well look around a minute."

Lew stepped to the hitching rail, which had fallen over. "Tied my horse here many a time. Don't seem possible. Everythin's different than it used to be. This was a goin' concern when I was here last time.

"The livery was right over here." Lew led Jake toward the livery, a heap of warped and twisted boards like gray waves on a stormy sea. The sun had set and there was a sudden coolness to the air; Lew rolled his sleeves down and hunted for the door on the side of the livery, found it lying flat, lifted the door to expose pale grass. He allowed it to slam shut, loose boards vibrated and then once more quiet descended.

Jake was staring off toward Venus when he first heard the whine; within minutes a Jeep, wound tight, came rattling off a sidehill. A cowboy was driving with a dog holding on to the passenger seat to avoid being tossed out. The Jeep skidded to a stop in front of a two-story building. The rancher jumped out and climbed the steps to the boardwalk, pounding sweat-soaked hat against his pants to beat out some of the dust. He noticed two strangers headed down the street but rather than wait he opened the door and went inside.

On the boardwalk Lew paused to pet the dog before going in. Jake pulled the door closed and stood there as Lew advanced across the room toward a naked dangling light bulb which pooled light around a gray-haired woman standing still as a mannequin. The cowboy was off to one side in the dark searching for the pork and beans.

"Not like I remember," Lew's voice rumbled as he looked around at the sparse shelves and the accumulation of dust. "Used to be a bar right here and upstairs was a couple of workin' gals. What happened, why's it dead?"

"Bullshit!" yelled the old woman suddenly coming to life, voice high-pitched and crackling like a Victrola. "Paradise Valley ain't dead. It'll come back to life. Them oil fellows is gonna make me rich. Wait and see."

The rancher, dumping a cardboard case on the counter, interjected, "Tillie might be right. She's lived around here longer 'n anyone else. All the others either died or moved but Tillie's too damn ornery to do either." He winked at Lew.

"Jimmy Crow, shut your trap," warned the woman, shaking a bony fist at him. "How many times do I have to tell you to take off that filthy damn hat. When you come in my place I want you to at least look like a civilized human being, even if you ain't." She hastily scribbled something on a slip of paper, handed it to the cowboy and told him, "Here's your receipt, now hit the road, sheep-dip."

Jim lifted the case of pork and beans on his shoulder and with a hearty laugh moved toward the door.

"That goes for you, too, Lew Minor," said the woman, turning her cutting voice on Lew. He removed his hat and stepped nearer her, asking, "How do you know my name?"

"I ought to. You worked for my daddy. I'm Tillie."

"Tillie Baldwin, sure I remember. Charlie Baldwin and me run mustangs together and you was a little girl in a red dress come runnin' out when we brought in the horses."

She was peering at the man Lew Minor had become when he gave her a hug as though she were still that little girl. She reeled back and bluntly asked, "How in the hell did you ever get so old?" And then tempering it somewhat, "Thought some bronc would have kicked you in the head and killed you way before now."

"Sure is good to run into someone I remember," beamed Lew.

"Well, it may be good for you but it's hell on a lady like myself. I look at you and know how old I must be. If I'm half bad a shape as you they might as well plant me in the cemetery. You sick?"

"I ain't been feelin' too hot as of late. My eyes is poor. I can't taste and barely can hear. My ankle bothers me pretty near all the time and so does my shoulder...."

"I remember your mother used to braid your hair, you looked like a little Paiute and now you're all grown, got your own business and ...."

"Don't I get to squeeze a word in edgewise? Come on, I got a beer joint in back. You can buy me a beer."

Jake joined Lew and they followed Tillie beyond the apron of light. She kicked at boxes stacked on the floor, reached another dangling light bulb and turned it on illuminating a short bar with a couple or three stools lined up along one side. She removed three Coors beers from the cooler and opened them. She tipped her bottle, reaching her lips to it like a baby robin begging for a worm and drank.

"How do we get to Double Square?" asked Lew, pushing back the beer and making room to lean.

"Why would ya wanta go there, all gone. Just a pile of rock. What broke Double Square and every other outfit in the country was the Taylor grazin' act. God damn government. Ever' time the government gets involved they screw it up. Range, there ain't no more range and there ain't no more Double Square."

"The hell you say. I remember runnin' mustangs.

Ride for days and never have to open a gate. Don't seem possible that could be gone.''

Jake finished his beer and abruptly announced they had to be going. He went to the door and waited, watched two old people embrace. It was another hour into Winnemucca and when they arrived and Lew awoke it might as well have been a foreign port. Blinking neon lights transformed the night into a dizzy spectacle of manufactured excitement, shadowy figures pulled slot machine levers, tourists whirled along the sidewalks like spinning tops from one gambling place to the next.

They rented a room at the Neda Motel and the next morning unsuccessfully tried to find the jewelry store where Lew had purchased his pocket watch. The building he thought it was turned out to be a hair stylist. After this latest disappointment Lew suggested they head for home.

A green highway sign welcomed them to Oregon and when Jake announced they were in Oregon, Lew instructed ''Pull over a minute.'' He got out and stood facing back toward Nevada where the Santa Rosa Mountains were the dominant feature. The mountains looked devoid of life and inhospitable but Lew had ridden for mustangs there and knew the hidden valleys and the secret draws.

''Well, ol' Nevada.'' He sighed. ''Guess this is it. I won't never see you again.'' A cloud sped over the landscape, covering Horse Hill and running across the open flats to Oregon Butte. That was enough and Lew turned his back on Nevada.

CHAPTER 22

Day after lonely day found Lew in the easy chair reliving the past. Beside him on the window sill was one of Kitty's Christmas cactuses that years before perished from neglect.

Lew was not qualified for social security or a pension and existed solely on income from selling a cow or a steer. But he had stopped replacing animals as they were sold and was down to a bull too crippled to climb on a cow's back, five sorry cows and three steers. When he could no longer see the numbers he owed on the bills that were sent him, he quit opening the envelopes. His utility bill was four months in arrears and service was disconnected but Jake settled the bill and paid the reconnect fee out of his own pocket.

"Lew, I hate to say it but you're goin' downhill. From now on I better take care of your finances," Jake told him and went on to say, "Your color doesn't look none too good. You're gettin' thin. Look at yourself. Hell, you haven't been eatin' like you should."

"I've just lived too goddamn long," claimed Lew, tired of enduring the hurting.

"Stop feeling sorry for yourself," reprimanded Jake. "You can't give up. What you need is a better diet. Probably make you feel a hundred percent better. From now on every Wednesday I'm going to pick you up and take you to dinner at the senior citizen center. That way you'll get a decent meal at least once a week."

That first Wednesday Jake anticipated Lew would

have forgotten, but to the contrary Lew was dressed up in wrinkled slacks and a western shirt with a bola tie featuring a silver horse shoe. He was seated on the first few inches of his chair but as soon as he saw Jake he was on his feet.

Lew seemed to relish the attention of the others at the senior center. Many of the folks came to shake his hand. He smiled absently at them because he could hear nothing of what was being said, only the whirring in his ears as if a windstorm were trapped there.

One Wednesday Jake was late so Lew drove himself to town. Pulling into the parking lot at the senior center he did not turn quickly enough and creased the side of a parked car with the bumper of his pickup truck. He was aware of what he had done and parked at the opposite end of the lot. When he got out he squinted about trying to determine if anyone had witnessed the minor accident. It did not appear as though anyone had, yet Lew, as he ate cole slaw and chicken pot pie, kept glancing toward the door expecting to have his accuser materialize there.

Jake stepped through the door and marched straight to Lew, Verna following. Jake put his hand on Lew's shoulder and wanted to know, "Why didn't you give me a half hour? You know I don't want you driving. Next time just wait, okay?"

Strangers, a man and woman, entered and stood just inside the doorway. Lew spotted them and, fearful they were the car's owners, reached for the apple cobbler and began spooning it into his mouth. Someone went to talk to the couple, then turned and pointed to where Lew, Jake and Verna were sitting.

The man was dressed in freshly oiled farmer's boots, a plaid wool jacket and canvas pants. His wife was red-haired and smiling. She had been looking forward to this moment for so long, knowing her husband was in seventh heaven. They went to Lew and he looked up at them over the rims of his glasses, running confused fingers through his thin gray hair.

The man was waiting for Lew's recognition but finally could restrain himself no longer and blurted, "I'd know you anywhere. Remember me? I'm John Thorpe." There was not a trace of recognition on Lew's blank face. "Johnny Thorpe. Chesaw. You and me, we slept in the same room. You worked for my dad."

Jake introduced himself, apologized for Lew noting, "He's hard of hearing, you have to speak slow and loud." To Lew Jake said, "An old friend. Johnny Thorpe from Chesaw."

John waited apprehensively, noticing the straight Roman nose that had been so identifiably Lew, was crooked now and not the solid facial feature it had been. The face looked as though it were soft putty. But the eyes were the same steely gray. There could be doubt about the eyes.

Lew seemed to be looking through John as if he were seeing something besides the seventy-year-old man. He was befuddled, sputtered, "Naw, Johnny Thorpe, he's just a kid."

Jake attempted to draw away some of the other man's embarrassment. "How long since you saw him?"

I don't know, let's see, must be all of sixty years anyway, sixty-four I think.

"I was a kid, Lew taught me to ride broncs, taught me the little secrets. I was a pretty fair rider, took second at Pendleton in '20. Wanted to win real bad 'cause I knew Lew had. After that I went to Hollywood, made movies, was Tom Mix's double. They paid me fifteen bucks a day and room and board. Boy, was I in the chips!

"In my prime I was a hot shot, but I tell you I could

never carry Lew's spurs.'' He glanced at Lew and Lew was trying to drink a glass of milk but pouring most of it down the front of him. "He was the best I ever saw. Neighbors used to bring in their rough stock when Lew was living with us and I never, not once, seen him get throwed.

"Sure did miss him when he got married. What ever happened to Edna Holmes?''

"Lew doesn't talk about her. All I know,'' Jake purposefully lowered his voice, ''she run off with a Mountie according to Lew, said it was a big mess. All I know is that when he moved back here in about '27 he was married to Kitty. She died a few years ago.''

CHAPTER 23

Lew's driver's license was set to expire on his birthday and Jake told him there was no need in his trying for another because the state would never give him one. "Just as well, too, 'cause you shouldn't drive."

"If they was to say so, well then it wouldn't be so bad. But I think I ought to give 'er a shot. If I don't make it then I'll stop drivin'."

Jake wanted Lew out from behind the wheel and privately comprehended the easiest way to accomplish that was to take Lew to the Oregon Department of Motor Vehicles in Enterprise. There was no way they would ever give him a license.

Jake informed the clerk at DMV, "Lew's got no business driving. He can't hear and can barely see. His reactions are real poor. He's liable to kill himself and someone else, too. Don't give him a license."

"Mr. Minor, will you please step this way," said the clerk, taking him by the arm and walking him slowly into another room and in front of a camera. "Look this way." There was a flash that blinded Lew and made him blink several times. The clerk began typing information from the previous license to a new license while the color picture was automatically developed. The face appearing was that of an exceedingly old man, ninety-three hard years etched on the skin. He was worn out and it showed in the sag of the jaw; the lip that was cut on the barb wire fence sat crooked. The picture was laminated to the license and the clerk asked for nine dollars.

"That's crazy!" barked Jake as he realized a new license was being issued. But the bureaucratic decision had been reached and the clerk stood firm in not allowing his authority to be usurped.

At the senior citizen dinner that day Lew showed his new license to almost everyone. He was proud of it, displaying it as though it were a very valuable prize. On the way home Lew broke away from thoughtfulness to announce to Jake, "I'm ninety-three years old, and they give me a brand new license. Ain't that somethin'. I'm not so sure I want to drive no more." He was thinking about creasing the car that time. "Yep, she's been a great ol' life, she has, and not without 'er ups and downs. A fellow never made a mistake, never lived. Can't believe I'm alive this long."

Jake said nothing. It had become impossible to carry on a conversation in the car with Lew because he could not hear. A few minutes dragged by and Lew mumbled to himself, "Ah, she's been a great ol' life, she has."

Jake told Verna that evening, "You know one of these days I'm going to go out there and find Lew dead. That'll be that. He might die in his sleep, might be an accident, I don't know, but sure as hell I'll be the one."

"Don't think about it," Verna told him.

"He told me today he had lived long enough. Said when he's dead and gone he'll be dead and gone just like he was never here at all. Suppose he could be right...."

"Jake, think about something else."

Jake was checking on Lew every other day. One day he opened Lew's mailbox and was surprised to find a letter; Lew got very little mail except advertisements addressed to occupant or boxholder. This letter was from the Pendleton Round-Up and Jake, suspecting it was good news, hurried to the house. Lew, sitting in his chair and looking out the window, had seen him coming and when Jake entered Lew hollered, "Come on in."

Jake was waving the letter excited about something, but Lew could not make out what he was saying until Jake shouted it in his right ear. "Open it up," Lew told him. "Tell me what she says. Maybe they want to do something special for me, after all it has been fifty years. Every bit of that anyway."

"Sixty-five years," corrected Jake, reading the letter. Lew waited for him to finish. "They want to induct you into the Round-Up Hall of Fame. Want to have a dinner in your honor."

"Write 'em back and tell 'em I'll be there."

Jake drove Lew over the Blue Mountains on the freeway. The Round-Up committee had made reservations for Lew at the Pendleton Travelodge. Jake got the room key, showed Lew to the door and went back after his luggage.

Jake planned on staying for the dinner, then driving home over the mountains and returning for Lew the following evening. Looking at his watch he told him, "Better get going. Dinner's supposed to start at seven and it's quarter to now."

Jake paid for his ticket at the door and told the woman taking money that Lew was the guest of honor. She motioned to a man who took Lew to the head table. Jake sat at the table in front of Lew. The room was already about half filled and laughter and voices mingled creating a hubbub of noise.

A woman and a man found Lew and took seats on either side of him. The woman pointed at a name tag she was holding. It read, "Hello my name is" and someone had written with a red felt pen "Lew Minor". She affixed it to Lew's coat lapel and Lew cocked his head trying to comprehend what it was and why it had been put on him. He concluded it must be an honor and looked up and smiled. Jake could see how poorly his dentures fit; Lew had been losing weight lately and Jake figured he weighed no more than 150 or 160 pounds. That was a long way from the solid 210 he weighed in his prime.

The couple led Lew to the buffet-style dinner; the man held a plate, the woman pointed at the various entrees and Lew nodded his head if he wanted any. After Lew was seated and began eating, the others were allowed to go through the line. Jake was one of the first and was finished with dinner when the emcee began to describe the action sixty-five years ago, the saddle bronc competition during the 1912 World Championship between Kelley, Acord and Minor.

During the speech there was a disturbance as two cowboys struggled to carry a saddle and saddle stand through the narrow passage between the tables to the front of the room. It was the Hamley championship saddle that Lew had ridden for so many years. Unbeknown to Lew, Jake had brought it over; the leather was shiny and the silver was polished. It was set in front of Lew and when he recognized it his face became animated because here was something concrete. It seemed as though the Hamley saddle had always been a part of him. He smiled broadly and his false teeth slipped sideways a little. He was drooling and when he became aware of it he wiped it away with a napkin.

Pictured in his mind was the way the saddle looked

on Til Taylor's horse that day he won it; the palomino horse, flowing tapaderas and silver trappings. The tapaderas he had taken off. The silver had tarnished over the years. The saddle had been ridden hard but it was still solid. Lew took heart seeing it.

The speaker was talking into the microphone, "Bronc riders don't come any better than this gentleman on my left. I hereby induct this saddle and the cowboy who rode it, Lew Minor, into the Pendleton Round-Up Hall of Fame. Ladies and Gentlemen, may I present the World Champion of 1912, Mr. Lew Minor."

There was a polite round of applause. Lew saw them clapping but did not realize it was for him. The speaker led him to the podium where he adjusted the microphone to Lew's height. Lew stood there swaying, raspy breath amplified by the loudspeaker.

"Where's Angel. Angel ought to be here," called Lew and his voice boomed over the PA system. He stepped back and the emcee stepped forward to tell the crowd that Angel was the horse Lew rode to the championship.

What he did not mention was that after losing to Lew, Angel escaped, ran wild for several years in the Blue Mountains before being located and brought back to perform at other Pendleton Round-Ups. Eventually, after years of faithful service, Angel developed fistulous withers and had to be destroyed. He motioned Lew back to the microphone and melted into the background.

"I'll bet none of you can brag it around you won the world championship sixty-five years ago." He tapped his breastbone. "I can."

The crowd laughed and clapped and Lew sat down. Then someone in the crowd stood and they all stood and cheered yesterday's hero.

After the dinner Jake returned Lew to his room at the

Travelodge. The railroad mainline ran directly behind the motel and as a train rumbled past Lew sensed the vibration and looked alarmed.

Jake shouted, "Train."

Lew nodded and announced, "Train come into Wallowa and it was never the same after that. It sure all changes in a hurry. I'm tired. I'm gonna go to bed."

Jake made sure that the shirt Verna had ironed for Lew was hung in the closet and that the shaving kit was by the sink and then departed. Lew slept straight through without awakening. In the morning he pulled back the curtain and it was drizzling. He dressed in the same clothes he had worn the evening before, shaved here and there with an electric razor and was combing his hair when the couple who had been his hosts the night before arrived and said they were ready to take Lew to the parade.

Lew was ushered to the head of the line of nervous horses, marching bands and girls twirling batons and helped into a buggy pulled by four miniature horses. He plopped himself on the rear seat alongside an ancient Indian woman dressed in beads and white buckskins. On the front and back of the buggy were signs proclaiming "King of the Cowboys and Queen of the Indians".

Along the parade route the miniature horses pranced, clicking metal to pavement in a rhythmic cadence. Onlookers applauded while photographers froze an instant of time for all time. Some pictures showed Lew tipping his hat, he was just sitting in others; the Indian woman waved in all of them as if her arm never tired. Pulling into the Round-Up arena they circled the track to the cheers of a crowd that had begun to gather.

The buggy was stopped in front of the reviewing stand. The old woman climbed down by herself but Lew needed help. The PA system blared, "Welcome to the 1977 edition of the Pendleton Round-Up. We will join together in singing the national anthem."

Lew did not comprehend the strains of the *Star Spangled Banner* and did not remove his hat until the colors were brought horseback to the front of the reviewing stand. Then he held his hat over his heart and tried to stand straight and keep from swaying. He thought he might lose his balance and fall, but that feeling passed.

A chocolate-dipped cloud spit rain, a drop struck the side of Lew's face and slid over the canyons and ridges of skin. Lew replaced the hat and wiped at the raindrop as though it were a tear.

"Not often do I have the honor of introducing a world champion but today I have the distinct pleasure to welcome Lew Minor, 1912 World Saddle Bronc Champion. Last night Lew was inducted into the Round-Up Hall of Fame."

Lew, standing slump-shouldered, became aware of rumbling vibrations and glanced at the crowd; they were standing and clapping. He waved his hat and they cheered more and he grinned and drank in this adoration. After months of sitting at home in front of the window so all alone and lonely, he reveled in the accolades. And then it was over.

A fat man wearing a new straw hat passed a beer to his partner and commented, "Probably biggest thrill that old fart ever had, winning that championship."

His buddy replied, "He's so old, if he took flowers to the cemetery there would be no sense him comin' back." The two giggled.

The rodeo was about to get underway and Lew was led to a box seat where he sat with the host couple. He was close enough to the track that he could almost see himself taking his victory lap. The roar of the crowd filled his mind. They were wildly tossing hats and cushions into the air without any regard where they would land. And he doffed his hat and saluted them.

In the arena, what seemed an endless number of entrants competed in team roping. Lew ignored the riders roping the small calves and stretching them out, to him the event did not belong with a rodeo. Instead he concentrated on recalling every last detail, every tortuous twist and turn and buck of his ride.

"Angel, you was a good ol' horse," he said aloud to himself at one point. The woman regarded him skeptically and then decided when he started answering himself she might do something, perhaps move to the other side of her husband.

"We roped hard-charging eight-hundred pound steers," Lew announced in his loud voice, giving a start to the woman. She recovered, saying, "Is that so?"

"It don't seem possible the way things have changed."

The woman told Lew the first go-around in the saddle bronc event was about to take place and pointed to a line of chutes. Lew squinted and coming into a fuzzy focus was the gate of chute number one swinging open, a blur of motion; seconds ticked past, pick-up men squeezed from opposite sides and the rider chose one, swung off the bucking horse and safely onto the ground, all in one easy fluid motion.

Lew tried to recall how many times Angel had passed in front of the main grandstand on their wild ride, muttered, "Angel was an awful sunfisher. He bucked and I thought he never would quit." And then turning to the woman, he explained, "We didn't use no chutes in them days. Saddled 'em right in the middle of the arena and crawled on. You rode 'em 'til they either quit buckin' or you got throwed. I was never bucked off in an arena in my life. That's a fact and I rode some rangy stock. By God, I did.''

The cool of the afternoon settled in Lew. He shivered and wiped at his nose, which had begun to run, with a kerchief. Each time he smeared at the nose the woman looked the opposite way.

Her husband was the one who noticed Lew's false teeth were chattering and suggested maybe they should go, but when Lew finally was made to understand he vehemently shook his head no and replied, ''I wanna see it all.''

Finally, in a lull in the calf roping, the man rose and signaled they were going. Lew had difficulty standing. His legs were asleep. The couple tried to assist him but he rebuffed their attempts and with sheer willpower moved along the walkway, holding onto the railing as he did. The man muttered privately to his wife, ''If I ever get that old, shoot me.''

Lew had the suitcase packed and was seated on the bed, elbows resting on thighs. When Jake got there he pounded on the door but Lew never heard or sensed it. Jake had to get a key from the office, emotions grinding his insides because he fully expected to find Lew dead. But instead he found Lew ready to go.

''How are you doing?'' Jake asked and Lew made a motion of helplessness that he could no longer hear. Lew had forgotten his clean shirt in the closet and his shaving kit so Jake packed them.

On the way out of town, Lew dabbed at his nose several times and sneezed once so hard that he loosened his dentures. He spit the teeth into his hand and put them in his shirt pocket. Jake turned to Lew with concern and remarked, ''Caught yourself a cold, huh?'' Lew did not hear.

On the long Cabbage Hill grade, near the top, Lew asked Jake if he would pull over. Jake turned off the freeway at the viewpoint. An uplifting wind carried the smell of stubble fields and freshly turned earth, but Lew could not smell it, only feel its feathery touch on his cheeks. He faced the wind; behind him cars zipped past and trucks churned uphill. Heads gawked at the old man standing before the long, steep incline. A youthful voice shouted, "Jump!"

Lew endeavored to focus on the undulating wheat fields. A cock pheasant screeched and from somewhere above in the gray sky a sonic boom crashed and splashed over the land. Lew hesitated a moment, drew a deep breath.

"Goodbye ol' Pendleton. Goodbye. I'll never see you again."

CHAPTER 24

Nig's ears twitched at the knowledge a car was coming and he lay savoring for a few more seconds the warmth of Lew's lap and then abandoned the spot, slipped through the open door and the torn screen and ran behind the house and hid. Lew felt him go and knew from experience that someone was there, most probably Jake, but he could not muster the strength to rise.

Jake kicked snow from his boots on the steps. He regarded the open door, tried to recall how many times he had told Lew to keep it closed because he was wasting energy. Two years ago Jake had put in an oil heater and he reminded himself to check the level of oil in the tank before he left. He found Lew in his customary position in the chair.

"How are you feeling?" asked Jake and Lew, knowing what the question would be, stated, "Not worth a damn. My strength has gone and left me." For emphasis the mantle clock chose that moment to run down, a subtle but obvious change. Jake looked around but did not perceive the clock had ceased to mark time.

The temperature in the room was not uncomfortable but Lew was wrapped in a blanket. Jake made the motions of rubbing his arms and asked if Lew was cold.

"Freezing," replied Lew. Jake got Lew on his feet and into the car. He drove to Enterprise where the doctor diagnosed pneumonia and arranged for a room at the hospital.

Four days after entering the hospital Lew was released feeling better than he had in months. But once again at home he reverted to a schedule of sitting, very seldom expending the energy it took to fix something healthy to eat. There were no longer any cattle on the ranch, they had all been sold. The chickens were gone, too, having wandered away when Lew forgot, days on end, to feed them. The coyotes had had a field day.

Jake came to check on Lew every day, usually in the early afternoon, and Lew would greet him with some disparaging remark like, "I don't know why I'm still alive," or "I've outlived my usefulness."

One Saturday Jake felt seized by a strange foreboding as he turned down Lew's lane. He felt it in his throat and tearing at his stomach. Was this to be the day, he asked himself, that he would find Lew and he would be dead? He tried to tell himself that might be the best but could not bring himself to easily accept such a point of view. He hoped with his heart it would not be today, some other day but not today.

Lew was not in the recliner and Jake moved quickly toward the bedroom. Perhaps he had died in his sleep. He hated to look but forced himself. Lew was not in the bed. That left the kitchen, Lew might be passed out on the floor and Jake hurried and the wood floors creaked. He was not there, that left the bathroom. It crossed Jake's mind that he had heard of old men having heart attacks and dying while sitting on the john. He had the sinking seasation that he would find Lew there. But Lew was not in the bathroom and as Jake passed the front room again he had to take a seat for a minute because he felt lightheaded.

Outside the wind was blowing. Jake became conscious of the plastic on the porch flapping, raced outside, located Lew, dressed in his beaver coat, halfway down the trail that once lead to the barn. Lew was unsteady on his feet, shuffling along bent over at the waist. Jake took hold of him, stretched Lew's arm across his shoulders and carried him to the car.

Lew looked dazed, as though he did not quite know what was going on around him. His limbs were trembling and he was not in control.

A nurse at the hospital in Enterprise pushed Lew down the hall in a wheelchair, past vacant faces and numbered doors. In a room several nurses undressed Lew, got him into a backless gown and into bed. A doctor arrived and told the RN to begin IVs at once.

In order to give them time with Lew, Jake went down town, had a cup of coffee and walked around. At one point he stepped in a shop and bought a small figurine of a horse that he took to Lew's room and put in the window sill beside the bed. Lew's eyes opened. Jake stepped near, patting his shoulder.

Lew bellowed, "I seen it all. By God, I seen it all."

The outburst seemed to rob him of his strength and he breathed deeply and regularly as though drifting into sleep. His eyelids closed. Jake noticed for the first time that Lew's arms were tied to the side rails with strips of sheets. He moved to untie them but a nurse stopped him, saying, "It's for his own protection. So he doesn't try to get up or hurt himself."

Jake went away after that and returned the next morning. Much to his surprise he found Lew with the bed in a sitting position, seeming somewhat alert. Jake came near the bed and slowly Lew turned his head, his speech slurred and thick. "Hello, Jake. Jake, take my Winnemucca watch. Somebody's tryin' to steal it." Jake took the watch from the drawer beside Lew's bed and placed it in his pocket. He turned back but Lew was already asleep. A nurse appeared, checked Lew's blood pressure and in alarm rang the emergency buzzer and cranked the bed flat. "You'll have to leave," she snapped at Jake.

Jake looked back, saw Lew's emotionless white face, and then the swinging door slammed shut. Would that be his last memory of Lew? His lonely footfalls echoed down the hall. Behind him a rush of people went into Lew's room but Jake never looked back. Selfishly he thought how he would have dreaded finding Lew dead. Maybe it would be easier if it happened in the hospital. He was not sure. He went to the lobby and felt like calling Verna but did not.

Two weeks passed with Lew's fragile conditon continuing to deteriorate. One morning, when Jake had come for his usual visit, a nurse stopped him outside of Lew's room and in a low voice meant only for Jake's ears she explained, "It's only a matter of time. He is not doing well. I'm sorry."

Jake opened the door and before him on the bed, covered by a white sheet, was the frailty of life that Lew had become. He was already dead in most regards, except for that strong heart of his that refused to stop beating. He had the glory of the past but no present, no future.

Time stretched. A sparrow sang joyfully. The lilacs bordering the hospital window were alive with purple blooms. A patron of the library returned an overdue book, sliding it in the book drop, rather than going in and paying the fine. Children, laughing and playing, swung on the jungle-gym in the schoolyard. The salesman at the appliance store sold a new washer and dryer to a couple from Imnaha. In the bar a horse was traded for five ton of hay.

Lew had stopped breathing. Jake rang the emergency buzzer and within seconds a doctor and several nurses appeared. The doctor barked instructions, "Respirator! Pulse! Blood pressure!"

Jake slipped through the door and impatiently began

pacing up and down the hallway, pausing each time he passed Lew's door, but always going on. He told himself that Lew had lived a full life, that he had had the opportunity to do those things he had wanted to. There was nothing more he could accomplish by holding on to the last shreds of life. It would be best for him to let go.

A doctor appeared, placed an arm around Jake's shoulders and consoled him, "It's over."

At that instant the Nevada sun dropped between clouds and sent a brilliant shaft of light to reflect off a pool of still water. The surrounding desert was tranquil and at peace with itself. A quivering, tentative muzzle broke the flat sheen of the water. A mustang drank and with thirst satisfied, he raised his tail and ran off through the sage, free and wild.

"He's gone," Jake breathed into the phone.

"It's for the best," said Verna, but she was crying, too.

On the morning of July 1, 1978, mourners cut across the grass of Wallowa Christian Church, leaving a trail in the dew. Most were old, some walking with the aid of canes or walkers and a few were pushed in wheelchairs.

With solemn faces pallbearers moved up the aisle and stood near the casket. An old buckaroo in the front row cried unashamed. The casket was open and Lew looked sound asleep and content in death. He was holding a brand new four-X beaver Stetson Jake had picked out. Jake closed the lid and the pallbearers started carrying the casket back down the aisle.

A chunky girl sitting on a stool began strumming a Gibson guitar. In a quavering Okie voice, high-pitched like a coyote calling its mate, she sang a fetching song, dry as sagebrush and sand:

> *In the hills of tomorrow, there'll be no sorrow*
> *Old friends you'll find in the hills far away.*
> *Travel on, on and on, through the hills of*
>   *tomorrow*
> *Where we all will be there some day.*

THE END

"I remember when I decided to write a book about Lew Minor," recalled Rick Steber. "It was a hot summer day and Lew and I were sitting on a bale of hay, leaning back against the cool of a log barn. Lew, who by then was an old man, told me the stories of his youth: breaking out horses for the Double Square outfit, doing time for cattle rustling, winning the World Saddlebronc Championship. . . . I wanted to write the book and depict the exuberance of youth and being the best in the world at something you truly loved, contrasted against the cold realities of old age, outliving your time and your usefulness.

"I interviewed Lew over a seven-year period. During that time his few remaining friends passed away. But Lew hung on, living alone on his ranch. He grieved at having to put down his last horse and when he could no longer care for his cows he sold them off, one by one, until all that remained was a flock of worthless chickens that he fed by hand.

"Day after day he sat in front of the window, a scrapbook of rodeo pictures on his lap and all those memories of the distant past so vivid in his mind they might have happened yesterday, patiently waiting for the end."

Rick Steber has written more than twenty books. He resides near Prineville, Oregon with his wife Kristi and sons Seneca and Dusty.